FDR'S MOVIEMAKER

FDR'S MOVIEMAKER

MEMOIRS & SCRIPTS

BY PARE LORENTZ

UNIVERSITY OF NEVADA PRESS

RENO : LAS VEGAS : LONDON

The paper used in this book meets the
requirements of American National Standard
for Information Sciences—Permanence of
Paper for Printed Library Materials, ANSI
Z39.48-1984. Binding materials were chosen
for strength and durability.

Library of Congress Cataloging-in-Publication
Data

Lorentz, Pare.

   FDR's moviemaker : memoirs and scripts /
Pare Lorentz.

      p.   cm.

Includes bibliographical references and
index.

      ISBN 0-87417-186-5 (acid free paper)

   1. Lorentz, Pare. 2. Documentary films—
United States—History and criticism. I. Title.

PN1998.3.L67A3   1992

791.43'023'092—dc20   91-38493

                              CIP

University of Nevada Press,

Reno, Nevada 89557 USA

Copyright © 1992

Pare Lorentz

All rights reserved

Designed by Richard Hendel

Printed in the United States of America

9 8 7 6 5 4 3 2 1

FOR ELIZABETH

Better go down upon your marrow-bones

And scrub a kitchen pavement, or break stones

Like an old pauper, in all kinds of weather;

For to articulate sweet sounds together

Is to work harder than all these, and yet

Be thought an idler by the noisy set

Of bankers, schoolmasters, and clergymen

The martyrs call the world.

—W. B. Yeats "Adam's Curse"

Before we were all seated, those of us who had not had dinner with the President before watched the President come through the door and wheel his way up to the front of the room in his wheelchair. Behind came two Episcopalian bishops dressed in velvet knee breeches both of them haranguing the President's mother, Mrs. James Roosevelt, about what she was going to do with her home in Hyde Park in her will. They were smoking long cigars that would have done credit to very prosperous movie producers.

The President spied me and interrupted the bishops' interrogation long enough to look at me and introduced me, saying "he's my shooter. He photographs America to show what it's like to our people" . . .

—Pare Lorentz

CONTENTS

Introduction : 1

Prologue : 3

A Young Man Goes to Work : 6

How I Became a Movie Critic : 17

Censored: The Private Life of the Movies : 20

The Bitter Years : 23

The Roosevelt Year : 27

How I Became a Moviemaker : 32

The Making of *The Plow That Broke the Plains* : 39

Script for *The Plow That Broke the Plains* : 44

The Making of *The River* : 51

Script for *The River* : 60

The Making of *Ecce Homo: Behold the Man* : 77

Script for *Ecce Homo: Behold the Man* : 83

John Steinbeck: A Working Friendship, 1938–1942 : 105

In Dubious Battle : 112

The Making of *The Fight for Life* : 116

Chicago : 132

The White House: New Year's Eve, 1939 : 149

The Making of *The Fight for Life,* Concluded : 159

Script for *The Fight for Life* : 164

Epilogue : 227

Appendix : 231

Acknowledgments : 235

Index : 239

The films of Parc Lorentz are acknowledged masterpieces of world cinema. They are groundbreaking documentary records of our country in the hard years of the Depression. And they are as meaningful today as they were then.

These films talk about the land and the rivers of America and what we Americans have done to them. And they talk about ways to address the problems we have created. They offer common sense solutions to serious ecological attacks on our most precious resources.

And in the halls of the legislature we still debate ground water protection and air pollution control. And in the halls of Congress we still debate acid rain legislation and toxic waste disposal. Mr. Lorentz, through these films, first focused national attention on massive regional problems and showed what the government of Franklin Delano Roosevelt was doing to correct them.

But what separates these films from other government films and from other documentary films is not so much the message, universal though it is, but rather it is the use of the medium itself as a tool for social change. More than simply a record of an event or a bland entertainment, these government documentaries combine images and music and words with such emotional force that they engage the senses and reverberate in the intellect.

It is the quality of these presentations that developed an audience and enabled them to be shown in commercial movie houses all across this country. And it is the clever montage of stock footage and fabulous original cinematography and the masterful use of an original score that make these productions such important technical achievements in the history of film. And it is the use of the medium as an art form combining verbal and visual and auditory poetry that set these films apart and placed their writer-producer in the pantheon of American film-makers.

William M. Drennen, Jr.*

*William M. Drennen, Jr., Commissioner, Division of Culture and History, Cultural Center, Charleston, West Virginia, at the First Annual Media, Literary and Visual Arts Conference of the West Virginia Division of Culture and History. Pare Lorentz was the first recipient of the MLV Lifetime Achievement Award, which was presented in the State Theatre of the Cultural Center after screening two of his films: "The Plow That Broke the Plains" and "The River."

I left my home state of West Virginia in the summer of 1925, departing from my maternal grandparents' house on Mulberry Avenue in Clarksburg attired in white linen knickers, driving my Uncle John's Model T Ford, and accompanied by the sheriff of Comanche, Texas. My Uncle John Ruttencutter, my mother's older brother, sent the sheriff from Texas to have me act as his guide and driver. The summer before, I had worked for my uncle in the southwestern states of Oklahoma, Arkansas, Louisiana, and Texas. He was the representative of a magazine called *Pictorial Review* and the head of their southwestern magazine distribution company, called Pictorial Service. Prior to that position he had worked for some years as the circulation manager for "Pa" Ferguson, who, besides being the impeached former governor of Texas, owned the Temple, Texas, newspaper, the *Telegraph*. (My adventures in the Southwest took place in 1924, the year "Pa" Ferguson successfully ran his wife, "Ma" Ferguson, for governor of Texas.) I had driven during the summer from Oklahoma City to Laredo, Texas, by way of new oil boom towns such as Smackover, Mexia, and Eldorado. As a result of this experience, both my uncle and the sheriff had full confidence in my ability to drive to New York City and environs.

In my nineteenth year, I had erratically completed my junior term at West Virginia University, and the purposes of my trip north were, first, to show the sheriff the big city—a chore for which I was highly qualified, as I had spent at least five days there attending university football games—and, second, to obtain gainful employment.

A few years later, having found "gainful employment," I was sitting late one night in Barney Gallant's Greenwich Village speakeasy with Mark Hellinger and Walter Winchell, exchanging anecdotes with Barney, when suddenly Mark turned to me and said:

Pare Lorentz (with bucket) prepares his Uncle John's Ford for the trip from his grandparents' house on Mulberry Avenue in Clarksburg, West Virginia, for the sightseeing trip to New York, with the sheriff of Comanche, Texas, looking on.

"That's a good name you made up for yourself. How did you think of it?"

Coming from a long line of monologuists on both sides of the family, I was, nevertheless, speechless. But as briefly as possible, here's the story:

I was born on Pike Street in Clarksburg, West Virginia, in a one-room apartment next to the Robinson Grand Theatre the night of December 11, 1905, the firstborn and only son of two young, handsome, and church-poor people: Alma MacTaggart Ruttencutter Lorentz and Pare Hanson Lorentz. My great-grandfather Jacob Lorentz was born of Palatinate settlers in Lancaster, Pennsylvania, on February 28, 1776, and he died in Lorentz, West Virginia, on April 11, 1866. Upon taking up a land grant in the Virginia wilderness given him by Governor John Tyler, he stopped by Tygart's Valley and married Rebecca Stalnaker, daughter of one of George Washington's captains, and established the hamlet which still bears his name in what is now central West Virginia.

My mother was descended from a long-lived and deeply devout Alsatian and Scot people, who took up land on the Ohio River border of Virginia in colonial times. Her parents, from whose home I departed in 1925, were named Sarah Ann MacTaggart and Greenberry Ruttencutter. They lived to celebrate their sixty-fifth wedding anniversary, and all the years of their lives they were tithers and devoted themselves to the health and education of their children and grandchildren.

In a way, Mark Hellinger was right; I did make up my name in that I was baptized in Saint Paul's Southern Methodist Church on Pike Street as Leonard MacTaggart Lorentz. I like the anecdote of the baptism. Reverend Smith "Daddy" Wade was a veteran combat chaplain of the 19th Virginia Volunteer Cavalry that had fought with Stonewall Jackson. He performed the marriage ceremony for my parents, and his only son, Harry Wade, married my father's oldest sister, Bess. Anyway, when Reverend Wade sprinkled me on the head with holy water, I reached into the crucible, got some water, and sprinkled him back.

There was a great argument with my mother over my name. First, my father, of course, wanted me named for him, but he had an Uncle Pare Boggess and a Cousin Pare Rapp, so the argument of the old aunts, etc., was that another Pare would be too many and too confusing. Next, they decided to name me after my father's older half-brother Joseph and add Lee for Robert E. Lee. My mother again stormed, because she had been nicknamed "Little Joe" because of her tomboy antics, including doing handstands on top of an oil derrick. Thus, finally the name Leonard was chosen for the New England Union Army branch of the family. MacTaggart was, of course, for my blessed maternal grandmother.

Anyway, when I started to write for publication, I took my father's name, although I wrote a few little squibs for *The New Yorker* under the name Leonard MacTaggart that first summer of 1925, the first year of *The New Yorker*'s existence. When I informed my father that I was going to use his name, he grumbled, "I have had enough things blamed on me," but as the years went on, he was quite pleased.

As for me and the sheriff, we spent a strenuous week together and for the first and last time I did a complete tourist's round of the city from Grant's Tomb to Coney Island to the Statue of Liberty to Staten Island—the whole bit. As an associate of Uncle John's, the sheriff was a dry-speaking, well-knit, civil gentleman. I never saw him again, but I hope he prospered and remained unshot.

Save to see my people, I never went home again.

A YOUNG MAN GOES TO WORK

I graduated from Buckhannon High School in the class of 1922 and wished to attend West Virginia University with several of my good friends who had been varsity players on our high school basketball and football teams (on the latter of which I was scrub quarterback). We were enticed by the new successful WVU football teams under "Fats" Spears. My mother strongly objected to my leaving home for the university because I was too young, so reluctantly I enrolled in my hometown college. As I was already a violin student at their music department and played in the college orchestra, I had sort of been going to my hometown college for several years.

That summer I was enticed by the U.S. Army posters announcing the first Student Army Training Camp at Camp Knox, Kentucky. The posters blared out, "Have a vacation at Uncle Sam's expense." My father let me fib about my real age by having one or two of his stalwart friends certify that I was eighteen years old instead of seventeen.

In the fall of 1923 I transferred to West Virginia University without much trouble even though my mother was distressed at my leaving home. I was accepted as a sophomore and, if they were somewhat erratic, my grades were pretty good on the whole. It had been assumed I would study law, as had my grandfather, so I put in for pre-law, which allowed students with good marks to take a law course in two years instead of three, the senior undergraduate year being given a credit of one year in law school.

It was the following summer of 1924 that I went to work for my Uncle John in the Southwest and for the first time saw the limitless horizons of the Great Plains, where I was to work for the U.S. government making my first documentary film eleven years later. During an earlier summer vacation I had worked for a brief time in a sawmill up in the mountains, but just as in the case of Mark Twain and the ore stamping mill, although they offered me over $150,000 a week to stay on, I quit.

File Corporal Lorentz, middle man in second row, Company A, Students Army Training Camp, Camp Knox, Kentucky, August 1923.

My father was a printer, and from boyhood I had done chores usual to a job-printing plant: numbering checkbooks, stapling, trimming, locking up forms, pulling and reading proofs, and feeding a Miller hand press.

Buckhannon, West Virginia, is a county seat and also the home of West Virginia Wesleyan College, and my father printed most of their work, producing some very handsome publications for them. He was better than an ordinary small-town printer. American Type Founders often sent him new typefaces with which to experiment after he won his two awards. The first award was from the American Printers' Association for his excellence in layout, and when I was seven years old in 1912 he was declared the best small-town printer in the United States by the *Inland Printer* magazine.

My father taught me typefaces, layout, and design, and, as I may not have another opportunity to report it, he was the most courteous, gracious, and selfless man I ever knew.

Because I was encouraged to be whatever my bent seemed to indicate, I competed for the school oratory prize and was on the debating team and took elocution lessons to improve my diction at West Virginia Wesleyan College under the dramatic coach Miss Mildred Little. (Many years later, she was in charge of the dramatic department at Sarah Lawrence College.) She cajoled me on stage until once I played Sam to Percy Ross's Penrod in the dramatic school play she put on at the college.

I also took violin lessons at the college. I had a patient, good teacher by the name of Spaulding, and I appeared in several student recitals and sawed away happily in the college orchestra at such epics as "The Bohemian Girl" and "The Prince of Pilsen."

Shortly after the Armistice, and while I was still in high school, June (nickname for Junior), the son of our next-door neighbor, a stern, well-to-do judge by the name of Ulysses Grant Young, bought a set of trap drums and persuaded two college musicians, Harold Salm, a pianist, and Slats somebody-or-other, a trombone player, and myself to practice jazz numbers in his mother's ornate music room. It was pretty daring to have a jazz combo in a college town that had been dry for forty years and that had an ordinance against public card playing and dancing, but because of the prominence of his family, June was able in time to book us for dances given by our elders. We were hired by the Eastern Star ladies and such groups.

I played the straight stand-up leader, and we would memorize our songs by going to the Whitscarver Undertaking Parlor, where they also sold Victrolas as well as caskets, and we would listen to the new Paul Whiteman records and then go home and rehearse.

When I got to the university there was a group already organized called the Old Gold and Blue Orchestra, and it played for good-sized fees. These were good men. The trap drummer—Fuzzy Knight— ended up with George Olson's orchestra in New York, where he did a comic act something on the order of Jimmy Durante's. Later he went to Hollywood, where he was one of the Three Mosquiters, who made dozens of motion pictures. Another good musician in that group was Paul Mason, who was in the orchestra that played at the Biltmore Hotel Cascades. The pianist, whose name was Nelson Maples, later formed the Nelson Maples SS *Leviathan* Orchestra.

There were also two men with Paul Whiteman's big band who were from my hometown of Clarksburg: Charlie Gaylord, a fiddler, and Skin Young, who could sing "Won't You Come Back to Our Alley Sally . . . Don't Say No" an octave higher than it was written (and not in falsetto, either).

Somewhere along the line I became much more interested in foot ball than in playing the fiddle. I never got in the big leagues with either profession, but I worked hard at both, particularly once I started getting strong and free of bugs.

When I went down to the Whitehall Building in New York City to take my physical exam before going to training camp in the Second World War, I had a wonderful, kindly old retired aviation doctor who did my examination, whispering so loudly in my game ear that you could hear him ten blocks away. As he rambled on asking me questions, he came to childhood diseases, and I answered, "Mumps, whooping cough, measles." Then I continued, "typhoid fever, diphtheria, second case of measles, appendicitis."

The old doctor put down his pen and looked at me in astonishment and said, "Good God man. Where were you born?"

When I said "West Virginia," he seemed to understand, but he was still shaking his head when I left his office. From the first time I came to New York City for what proved to be a permanent move until I had a kidney stone removed in 1955 at Johns Hopkins in my fiftieth year I never saw a doctor again for any reason save when I was forty and had to have reading glasses.

Before I left the university I was named editor of our comic magazine, the *West Virginia Moonshine*, by the graduating senior staff, which consisted of two of my best friends, Joe Savage and Jack Ratcliff. I had worked with them for two years and had been their chief editorial writer. During that time I helped get the magazine banned from the university campus by order of the governor of the state, and I was twice suspended and once expelled because of my editorials.

These, then, were my qualifications for employment that wild, frenetic year of 1925—the year of the start of the Coolidge bull market and of the ascendancy of Al Capone and the mobsters. I knew a little bit about music and quite a bit about jazz music. I knew my way around a printing office, and I had some knowledge of life in the mountains and the conditions in the lumber camps and coal towns. I was a voracious reader and learned to use public libraries. I discovered early on the British critics, my favorite being G. K. Chesterton.

I perhaps have dwelt in too much detail about my not too unusual youthful activities, but ten years later, when I started to rove the country with a camera crew to work with Dust Bowl migrants, tenant farmers, factory workers, engineers, and national forest and park rangers, knowledge of how to keep your manners with working people came in handy.

As for myself, I weighed in at 135 pounds, not yet having got my heft. I was just short of five feet eleven inches. I was equipped with an old Oliver typewriter, a fiddle, and one blue suit, and I had slightly under two hundred dollars in the bank and no source of obtaining any more save by earning it. I did, importantly, have the security of knowing that I could always go home to simple, good food, clean linen, and a warm welcome.

Peering through the thick mists of time, I cannot remember all the details of those first few weeks of trying to get a job. I know that I headed first for the *New York World* newspaper offices, as all the brilliant columnists and critics and reporters of that great newspaper had made it our bible at the university, and I do remember being thrown out of the reception room by a fang-toothed office boy before I hardly began to speak. I tried to get a job as a movie usher at the old Strand Theatre and was outraged when I was turned down—probably because I was not big or surly enough.

I was disappointed in one of my heroes, Joseph Conrad, when after a week of presenting myself to the maritime hiring hall on Greenwich Avenue, where I had gone to get a mandatory life-saving certificate, I was not only unable to run away to sea, but also was thrown bodily out of the hall to the accompaniment of some unpleasant comments about college boys and their habits.

Somewhere, someplace, I wrote some anecdotes and little squibs of buffoonery and took them to a new magazine that had just started publication in February of that year: *The New Yorker*. The editors bought some of them and gave me a by-line, and one of the short pieces was carried on the front page. Three of the young men helping to edit the new magazine—Ted Shane, Corey Ford, and Phil Wylie—had also come from college humor magazines, and they were friendly enough to urge Harold Ross to employ me. That first meeting he wound up saying he had enough humorists on the staff and what he needed was a New York club man who was listed in the social register. (Subsequently he found such a man in Ralph Ingersoll.) At different times, three people urged Ross to employ me as his movie critic: Katherine White (Mrs. E. B. White), Robert Sherwood, and Robert Benchley.

During our last work interview, Ross terminated the conversation by saying, "I hate movies."

I answered, "Then why in hell do you run a movie column in your magazine?"

I sold a few more little pieces to *The New Yorker*, but by August, time and money were running out. I either had to find a permanent job or go back to the university.

Because of our college magazine, I knew of the Four A's—the American Association of Advertising Agencies—and my very first week in the city I had registered with them. I stopped by regularly to ask a petite, dimpled, pleasant lady who ran the reception room if she had found any work for me.

As a last hope before returning home to West Virginia, I stopped by to see her, and she indicated a chap who just was leaving the office and suggested I talk with him. It turned out he once had been editor of the Cornell comic magazine, *The Cornell Widow.* As we walked up Park Avenue, he told me he had just quit his job as editor of a house organ, *The Edison Sales Builder,* to go to work in China for the Standard Oil Company of New Jersey. He suggested I go across the river to Harrison, New Jersey, and take over his old job.

By now I figured my youth and inexperience were against my finding any job in the big city, so before going to New Jersey I typed out a new work sheet. This time I not only indicated my actual qualifications and my new fame as a *New Yorker* magazine author, but I added a few more qualifications and stated that I had worked, among other places, for the *Charleston, West Virginia, Gazette, Collier's Magazine,* the *Montgomery, Alabama, Gazette,* and other distinguished journals. To clothe myself in my new maturity I went by Finchley's haberdashery shop and bought a stiff-bosomed shirt and a walking stick. Thus fortified, I took the Hudson tubes to Harrison, New Jersey, to the offices of the Edison Mazda Lamp Company.

The appointment was arranged by the Four A's. When I arrived at the company reception rooms, I was disheartened to find almost a dozen other aspiring editors on hand. We gave our applications to the receptionist, and each man was led out of the room and never returned until, finally, my stiff-bosomed shirt wilted by the oppressive August blanket of hot, foul New Jersey air, I found myself alone.

It was well after five o'clock. The receptionist had gone for the day, and I started to drowse from heat and boredom when the door banged open and a big, burly recognizable mountain man scowled at me for a minute and then bellowed: "You silly bastard, can you read and write?"

After scrutinizing me again, he said: "P.S. You get the job."

McIver took me to his office, brought out a bottle of gin, filled two water tumblers half full, sprinkled some warm water on top, and we became acquainted.

McIver was from North Carolina and he had been a major in the U.S. Marine Corps. He was vice-president of the company in charge of advertising. He informed me that all the other candidates he had interviewed were related to company officials and had no qualifications for the job. I always felt he hired me because I, too, was from the hills and because I was the most astonishing liar he had ever met.

During the year I worked as editor of the house organ, *The Edison Sales Builder*, I gave McIver a full measure of service, but I also more than once almost cost him his vice-presidency. I became competent in my job but fretted to myself as I gradually comprehended the hypocrisy and chicanery practiced by my employers. Some items:

Thomas Edison had long since sold all his light bulb patents outright to the General Electric Company, but I was frequently urged to mention his name in my publication and to try to indicate to the dumb clucks, which is how the sales department characterized my fellow peasants, that he personally made each Edison Mazda Lamp bulb with his own hands.

The Edison Mazda Lamp Company was totally owned by General Electric, which owned also the National Mazda Lamp Company in Cleveland. I met once in a while with the editor of the house organ of the National Mazda Lamp Company, and we were given to understand that we should try to indicate that we were bitter competitors. When I would ask questions about the true ownership of the National Company, I was told that there was a lawyer named Samuel Untermeyer who about once a month threatened to investigate General Electric on the grounds that it carried on illegal monopolistic practices, and therefore we had to pretend the two lamp companies were competing in order to avoid unfavorable publicity.

My magazine was printed in Schenectady at a big printing plant owned by General Electric. As it was an open shop, the printers wouldn't work overtime or hand-set some of my fancy layouts unless I came up with my work and helped them put the magazine to bed. I was at home, of course, in a printing shop and I got along well with the men.

I came to know several head engineers, and I introduced myself to Dr. Charles Proteus Steinmetz, the wonderful, crippled little chief research scientist for General Electric. It was because of talking with Dr. Steinmetz that I got McIver in real trouble.

Herbert Hoover was at that time secretary of commerce, and he was the favorite government spokesman of the private utility companies. One day in Atlantic City he made a speech to the Edison Electronic Institute, pontificating about the coming of superutilities and indicating that in a short time there would be only a few such supercompanies in the country and that power would be run from the Atlantic to the Pacific oceans for practically nothing.

After reading that speech, I called on Dr. Steinmetz the next time I was in Schenectady and asked him whether Mr. Hoover was correct in his predictions. The good doctor said the speech was utter nonsense—that at that time the transmission of power represented about seventy percent of the total cost of electricity. He added that a community steam generating plant probably was the most efficient and economical way we had to make electricity.

I wrote a sparkling editorial for my next issue sneering at Mr. Hoover and quoting Dr. Steinmetz. An official of the company chanced to read my editorial and called a meeting of the board of directors. They summoned McIver and gave him a real going-over and instructed him to correct this grievous misinformation I had given to our readers. If I hadn't been so low down in the chain of command, I probably would have been on my way out of the building for good that day. McIver bellowed at me for a while, but I wouldn't write a retraction unless he could get Dr. Steinmetz to reverse himself, and neither of us did anything about the matter.

Not long after this incident, I went back home for a visit, and my father told me about the takeover of a little steam plant which was owned by members of the community and local banks. There was resentment and obviously there had been kickbacks, but I wasn't interested in the scandal but for the fact that not long after the interstate conglomerate utility took over the plant, they cut down the famous shade trees on Main Street to put up modern light poles and, of course, raised the rates. A few years later I wrote an article entitled

"Public Service" for *Plain Talk* magazine about the devouring of our little hometown steam plant.

Sometime during that year we received instructions to fill *The Edison Sales Builder* with lyrical praise over the coming of a new GE inside-frosted light bulb. On one of my trips to Schenectady I asked one of our chief engineers to explain to me the real virtues of this new miracle product so that I might write sensibly about it. He informed me that the truth was that this inside-frosted bulb was not as good a product as those we had been manufacturing. Because of the difficulty of inside frosting, the bulb did not have a very long life, and it didn't give as good a light as the old bulbs.

"Why," I asked naturally, "are we going to make it?"

He explained that the Edison patents were due to run out, so other companies might begin to manufacture light bulbs. We were, therefore, going to put on an enormous national publicity campaign for our new product because we owned the exclusive patent rights to it.

Again I wrote another vigorous editorial indicating that our great new light bulb didn't glow too brightly. My magazine, of course, went to all GE dealers and sales departments, and this editorial caused quite an uproar in the head office. (I never have understood why I wasn't fired that time.)

We ran a full-page cartoon each month in the magazine. My cartoonist, Phil Rosa, was the art editor of *Judge,* and through him I met the editor-in-chief, Norman Anthony, and his merry crew. McIver and I would meet with this happy-go-lucky group several times a month, and I began to send Anthony little comic pieces, many of which he bought. McIver was pleased to see my name in print in a national magazine, comic or not, and he took a fatherly, tolerant attitude towards my extracurricular work. He also allowed me a great deal of latitude in my selection of assignments, considering the fact that what I was supposed to do was to help sell Edison Light Bulbs.

Two expeditions are still vivid recollections. The first was in the summer of 1925, when hoodlums, vandals, gangsters, and sneak thieves had just about taken over Philadelphia. The town fathers finally created a special police commission job and employed the First World War Marine Corps hero General Smedley Butler to be the commissioner. I read in the newspapers that he was using special light signals from the city hall tower to alert his special corps of policemen. He had evidently figured out there were only six hundred honest cops on the whole force and had made them into a combat brigade. I wrote him and to my astonishment was invited to Philadelphia to interview him about his light system and his activities in general. He was a man who was not unpleased by publicity. He was polite, although profane and loud, and I had a very pleasant day with him.

After I wrote the article and proudly presented it to McIver, I was chagrined when he said proudly, "You know, he was my commanding general in France."

The second and much more exciting commission was in New York City. I had attended the Ziegfeld Follies once or twice, and I suddenly realized how much lighting was used there for special effects. Being that I was not yet twenty-one years of age, those chorus girls were enough special effects for me, but I went to see Bernie Sobel, Ziegfeld's press agent, and asked how about doing a piece for the magazine. He was very enthusiastic and said that I could work from the wings, where he thought I would get the best view of the activities backstage.

What a week! Besides the beautiful women, there were W. C. Fields, Will Rogers, Ray Dooley, Phil Silvers, and some really good singers and dancers.

Rogers used to lasso famous people in the audience and bring them on stage to make a short speech and give a bow to the audience. I recall one night he lassoed Charlie Chaplin. After the show was over, he sat on a trunk fascinating the chorus girls (and me) with accounts of Charlie's beginning and his habit of depositing money in all sorts of banks and his real hatred of the United States because his mother had epilepsy, and when he sent for her, they kept her on Ellis Island for examination and then refused permission for her to come to America and shipped her back to England—this according to Will Rogers.

I met and talked with Chaplin several times when I became a moviemaker and worked in Hollywood, but he never mentioned his mother one way or another, and I, of course, never brought it up.

After I had worked for McIver for almost a year, I asked him for a raise. I had started to work for him at thirty-five dollars a week, and that is where my salary remained. McIver explained that it was impossible to give me a raise because I was part of a large group of employees on one wage plateau, and we would be raised up to a higher level all at one time. I countered by pointing out that I worked nights and sometimes weekends and that I didn't feel that I belonged to one great group because, after all, I was an editor. He offered to rig up a spurious field trip and let me take a long vacation home at company expense. I told him that was dishonest and that I wanted a raise.

Shortly after this interview, Norman Anthony offered me a job with *Judge* magazine, and I accepted as quickly as I could get my breath. Anthony was kind enough to warn me that *Judge* was on the verge of bankruptcy and that I might have a very short working life with him, but I couldn't have cared less. I had achieved my first objective: I had written myself out of New Jersey and into New York City.

When I told McIver I was leaving, he did his best to dissuade me. I remember he kept saying, over and over, "Stick with me and you'll wear diamonds."

McIver and I remained good friends. Four years after I left him, and in the depth of the Depression, *Scribner's* published my second serious article, "A Young Man Goes to Work," which was a reflection of my experiences working for a giant corporation. The reactions to this short article were fairly dramatic. I wish we had saved the letters. Dozens of young engineers wrote to *Scribner's* saying that they were married and were stuck in corporate boxes unable to move upwards and asking the editors or the writer to tell them what to do.

The second reaction was indeed dramatic. At that time I was living in a fourth-floor attic apartment on Eleventh Street. One night as I was working at my typewriter I heard what sounded like the thunderous approach of a rhinoceros on the creaky stairs. My old boss, McIver, was, as I have said, a big, burly man, and when he came crashing through my door, he was a big, burly, drunken man. He had a half-dozen copies of *Scribner's* under his arm, and he flung them across the room and announced that he had resigned his job and that he had sent copies of my article to all the directors of the General Electric Company with a denunciation of them and their employment policies, together with a statement that I represented one of the many young men he had lost simply because General Electric was so niggardly with money.

I lost track of McIver after that, but I know he married his patient, gentle, bespectacled secretary and moved to Hartford, Connecticut, where he either established his own electrical company or took over as head of a small specialty firm.

From 1926 until 1941 I had a by-line regularly either once a week or once a month, and for a while in 1932, every day, but I never did hear from McIver.

He was a good friend.

When I first went to work for *Judge* magazine, there was a wonderful, kind, gentle, experienced journalist named William Morris Houghton who wrote the editorial page and, at times, reported on movies. He had been the editor of *Leslie's Illustrated Weekly* during the First World War. He had been on the old *Daily Mail* before that and had been a correspondent in the war. I believe his father was once president of Bowdoin College and that the elder Houghton had been for a year tutor to Prince Hirohito, the now departed emperor of Japan. Bill Houghton was a good man who was against the Ku Klux Klan and for the repeal of prohibition.

One of the many banks that owned the hundreds of thousands of dollars' worth of notes on *Judge* magazine sent a representative and demanded that Houghton be fired because of his editorial stand against the Klan and for the repeal of prohibition on the grounds that it was hurting the sale of the magazine in the southern states. In a rage when this happened, my editor, Norman Anthony, appointed me as movie critic of *Judge*. (I think Anthony made me his movie critic more to get back at the bank than because of his admiration for my unproven writing ability.) That was in the summer of 1926.

The legend around the office was that *Judge* once printed a cover of President McKinley in shirtsleeves and carrying a dinner pail, the drawing being that of a huge giant of a man and the caption being one that McKinley used in his presidential campaign: "The Full Dinner Pail." It was said that the magazine had been bought as a result by Standard Oil of New Jersey and that in its generous way the oil company had requested a number of banks to accept notes or stock and return notes or something having to do with Standard Oil's selling the magazine to the William Green Printing Company, which, with its tin-roofed plant over off Eleventh Avenue in Hell's Kitchen, is where I first went to work for them.

Bill Houghton was not only a former editor, a war correspondent, and an editorial writer for *Judge*, but he had also been a classmate at Harvard University of Ogden Reid, publisher of the *New York Herald Tribune*. The day after the bank fired Bill, he was immediately employed as an editorial writer by the *Herald Tribune*. He also, along with his best friend, Clive Weed, put me up for membership in the Players, remarking that he and Clive were tired of buying me drinks. Bill ended his working days on the *Herald Tribune* and disappeared from the Players shortly after the *Herald Tribune* disappeared. He was a fine and decent man.

When I began as staff critic at *Judge*, I was not a movie buff or movie fan. However, by 1926, among other things Hollywood started making feature films of the great comedians. Chaplin already had made his first full-length movie. I think you will find *Shoulder Arms* came before I became a movie critic. I think you will find Douglas Fairbanks had made his magnificent silent movie, *The Thief of Bagdad*, before I became a movie critic. In New York City during my first years as a critic there was a showing of the Russian film *The End of St. Petersburg*, directed by Pudovkin, which, by the way, I think is a greater picture than those two early Russian movies made after the Communist Revolution: *Ten Days That Shook the World* and *Battleship Potemkin*. These are the two most usually cited as the greatest of the early Communist Russian spectacular productions.

The End of St. Petersburg was exhibited by Selwyn on Broadway in a legitimate theatre, where he sold reserved seats for two dollars or five dollars, I forget which. This was an unusual event in those early days.

I didn't go into the physics, the theory of light and contrast, as Steichen did in his youth. But I was interested in the form and the craft so sufficiently that in time some of the best of the Hollywood directors spoke tolerantly of me, and in time a few became very good friends.

Probably the one incident that led me to study the craft of motion pictures in earnest and to consider myself a responsible critic occurred shortly after my review of F. W. Murnau's *Sunrise*, which he made for William Fox (*Judge*, October 15, 1927). I will not quote from the review except that I stated toward the end that my theory was that William Fox would not let Murnau end the film in the tragic manner, as does the novel from which the film was made, *A Trip to Tilsit*.

Some years ago I bought the rights to quote from anything in Glendon Allvine's valuable and amusing book about William Fox entitled *The Greatest Fox of Them All*. Somewhere in the book he states that Mrs. William Fox forced Murnau to change the original sad ending of *Sunrise* into the almost low comedy with which it now ends.

Anyway, shortly after my review, a stocky, well-dressed, if European-looking, man came into my cubbyhole under the tin roof of *Judge*, clicked his heels together in a Germanic manner, bowed, and said, "Murnau has sent me to tell you that you are the only critic in America who understands what he tried to do in *Sunrise*." He clicked his heels and bowed and took off before I could get his name. I was at that time not yet twenty-two years old.

Because of my feelings about big corporate behemoths, I was impressed one morning with an open letter to the governor of New York State, Al Smith, which was published on the front page of the *New York Times* and signed by an attorney named Morris L. Ernst. I wrote him of my concern about giant utilities and said I would like to meet him. He very graciously replied promptly and invited me to dinner and talk at the Breevort Hotel in Greenwich Village. A slight, swarthy, staccato-talking man, Morris at that time represented many of the most famous authors in the city as well as being an attorney for several of the most reputable publishing houses. He also was engaged in several famous literary censorship fights, including his successful effort to have James Joyce's *Ulysses* allowed through U.S. Customs.

At our first meeting I told Morris that I wished to write a two-volume exposé of public utilities, and having read the news accounts of Al Smith's fights over the hydropower rights on the Saint Lawrence River, I felt he, Morris, might arrange for me to meet and talk with the governor about the matter.

Morris didn't laugh outright at me, although, considering the fact that I was neither a lawyer nor an engineer, that save for my little pieces of buffoonery I had never had any work published, and, finally, that I was not yet twenty-two years of age, it must have seemed rather a preposterous proposition to him. He didn't laugh, but he did engage in a habitual chuckle and pointed out the enormous scope of the proposed work. Then he turned to me suddenly and said, "Why don't we write a book on movie censorship?"

Ernst had more than a passing interest in the subject of censorship, as recently he had had a book published for the general public as well as for lawyers dealing with the history of, and the Anglo-Saxon laws of, libel. Entitled *To the Pure*, it is the most comprehensive and readable book on the subject I have ever read.

To this day I don't know how much of *Censored* is mine and how much is his, but in general it was agreed that I should write about movies and he would write about censorship and the laws, an obviously sensible arrangement.

One problem perplexed me for a while and that was how to get at the state censors, as I had neither the time nor the money to interview them myself. Finally I hit upon a simple solution: I bought copies of the most reputable out-of-town newspapers for a week running and studied the writing of the by-line reporters. I then wrote a few of them, including one each on the *Kansas City Star,* the *Saint Louis Post-Dispatch,* and the *Baltimore Sun,* and asked them if they would interview their home state censors and charge me newspaper space rates for their work. I suggested also that they represent themselves as being reporters from *The Christian Endeavor* magazine, the *Christian Science Monitor,* or some such religious publication, because that way they were more likely to obtain candid interviews.

They all accepted, their interviews indeed were revealing, and they charged very modest sums for their work.

That was a happy summer. I visited Morris and his family in Nantucket to work with him on the final draft of the book, and there was much laughter and not one sharp elbow during our association, although Morris did protest mildly about the epilogue I wrote; he felt it was a facetious conclusion. (He did not protest strongly and we included it. Reading it now, a generation suckled on electronic pap may agree with Morris that it is facetious. I think that, written almost half a century ago, it was quite prescient.)

When I finished the chapter on Will Hays, the "Bishop of Hollywood," I asked Morris to read it to see if I had libeled the gentleman. He read for a moment and then, his eyes sparkling, said: "Let's get him to sue us for libel! I'll defend us, and then we'll be able to get him on the witness stand so I *finally* will be able to cross-examine him." Forthwith Morris indicated a few phrases he felt to be libelous per se.

At this late date I have no desire to exhume the dirty linen of Will Hays, a man I consider to be a member of the jolly band of thieves who took control of our government with the ascension of Warren G. Harding to the presidency. He was a conniving, sanctimonious Indiana Presbyterian elder who was the bag man in the Teapot Dome affair. He was postmaster general under Harding and extricated himself from association with the gang by becoming the chief magistrate of the motion picture industry. One assumes he is busy stuffing ballot boxes in hell.

A few days after our book appeared and was reviewed favorably, a man on the National Board of Review called and asked me if I would meet with him and a delegation from the board. We held our conference in a shabby tavern in the theatrical district, and, after a few polite formalities, they unfolded their proposition. Mr. Hays had for some time been thinking that the movie industry deserved a high-toned expensive magazine devoted to only the most artistic productions. He had for some time been searching for an editor worthy of such a magazine, and he was prepared to pay him twenty-five thousand dollars a year. Finally he had found his man—me.

After I finished laughing and drinking and vice versa I left the delegation morose and drunk as hungry mourners at a wake and went to see Heywood Broun at the *World-Telegram* to inform him that Mr. Hays had offered me twenty-five thousand dollars to edit a nonexistent magazine. (Broun had written the excellent and thoughtful preface to our book *Censored*.) Heywood wrote a rollicking column about it which appeared the next day, but that was the last we heard from Mr. Hays, and no such magazine ever came into existence.

Will Hays didn't sue us, but he did offer me a job.

Looking back, it was extremely gracious of a successful attorney and author to take a young and untried author as his writing partner.

I remember the beauty of the October afternoon in 1929 in New York City when I walked out of Morris L. Ernst's office with an advance check from publisher Cape and Smith for six hundred dollars. Morris had given me the check after I delivered the finished manuscript of *Censored: The Private Life of the Movies.*

I bought an afternoon paper, and there was a black wartime headline announcing the crash of the New York Stock Exchange prices that day. I had never been far enough ahead to purchase any stocks or bonds, and I had for some time been skeptical of an economic system that allowed waiters and hotel porters to purchase stocks on margin and to repurchase stock on their uncashed credit accounts. I had figured there was going to be a day of reckoning, but I didn't have any concept of what a tragic era would be like.

I had various jobs between the fall of 1929 and May 1935, when I first became a consultant to the Resettlement Administration. It was a time of fading life for good magazines, some of which I had contributed to, and it was a period in which many publishers failed to realize the impact of the new medium, radio.

The *New York World* newspapers, morning and evening, closed down in May 1931, and shortly after that event I was at a cocktail party given by a talented and jolly illustrator named Russell Patterson. Without announcing himself, a stern-looking Irishman came up to me and said, "I've been looking and asking all around how I could get in touch with you. I'd like to talk with you right now." His name was Joe Connelly and he was the head of the Hearst King Features Syndicate. He took me over into a corner and said, "Mr. Hearst wants to hire you as movie critic on the *New York Evening Journal.* What are your terms?"

I told him I didn't want to work for a Hearst newspaper. He said it was too noisy for us to talk business, there were too many drinks flying around, and he asked if I could come out to his home in the suburbs, where we could relax and talk at length.

By asking around, I discovered that Hearst was attempting to make the *New York Evening Journal* more than just a blood-and-sex sheet and was hiring literary people in an obvious attempt to attract the abandoned *New York World* readers. I had made up my mind what I would settle for and had written a formal letter to Joe Connelly which I took with me when I went out to his house. He had a red-haired, green-eyed wife with two well-behaved and well-dressed young children whose manners indicated a real master sergeant type of mother, but she was courteous enough to me, and I liked their comfortable home and pleasant grounds.

What I had written Joe was that I would work as movie critic providing: (1) I would not have to review any movie in which Marion Davies appeared unless I wished to. (2) I would receive an assistant to do the housekeeping work of pasting up announcements, running a program guide, and answering nonsensical mail. (3) I would be allowed to go to Europe and look at the movie industry in France and England and particularly to meet René Clair in France and Alfred Hitchcock in England. Finally, he could set the salary.

Joe looked frightened after he read the first paragraph about Miss Davies and bellowed at me that obviously he couldn't sign any such statement. He said he'd give me a contract. I told him that he knew a contract was worth very little with Mr. Hearst, as few writers had the money to employ lawyers and go to court against such a rich man.

I also told Joe that I wanted to get married and have two weeks off in France for a honeymoon. He was rather startled, but he agreed because he said he and his wife were also going to France to do some work for Hearst. One idea he was supposed to pursue was to convince the French government to rent the Eiffel Tower to Mr. Hearst so he could use it as a radio broadcasting transmitter.

Joe then said he would see that I got three hundred dollars a week and expenses and an assistant (Rose Pelswick, who already was working on the theatrical page of the *Journal*), and he agreed that I could go to Europe as specified and that he would look forward to seeing me in Paris.

The next day I purchased a pair of English shoes and a good watch and made arrangements to marry the actress Sarah Richardson Bates, whose stage name was Sally Bates—not necessarily in that order of importance. The marriage took place in the home of Sally's widowed mother in Oswego, New York, and we sailed on the *De Grasse* early in August.

I did meet René Clair in Paris and had a fine time talking with him, and I did meet Alfred Hitchcock and examined the movie facilities at Elstree. The electricity was off at the time at Elstree, so they could not show me their new revolving stage. The utility company hadn't been paid, so they were paralyzed for the moment. Also, the crippled Welsh chancelor of the exchequer announced over the radio that England had gone off the gold standard, and besides that, it was broke.

The government resigned, and gleefully my host told me the king would have to come back from Scotland, where he had been grouse shooting, to occupy Buckingham Palace according to British law. He said we should go over and watch the changing of the guard, which is another ceremony required when the government fell or quit.

My host was a little, rotund Scot named Percy Bushwea who had enlisted in the Gordon Highlanders in August 1914 and for all his size had become a Lewis machine gunner and had been awarded the Victoria Cross after he had been wounded the fourth time.

We hardly had arrived in London when Mr. Hearst and his entourage, including lady friends of Marion Davies and Joe Connelly and his wife, all were summarily told to leave France. Apparently the Hearst papers had published some presumed French state documents implying that the French had engaged in espionage in Mexico during the past years. I don't know whether they were forged documents or real documents, but anyway, the whole Hearst delegation was ordered out of the country.

Joe called me at the Savoy, where we were staying, to say that I had been invited by Hearst to join them for a long weekend at Hearst's castle in Wales. I replied that I didn't want to be obligated to him socially while I was an employee and trying to write independent of any influence other than my own beliefs. Also, my wife had gone to visit family acquaintances in Wales, and I thought it would be awkward for me to be living in a castle with Hearst while she went sailing with her mother's friends.

I got along very well with the managing editor of the *New York Evening Journal*, Bill Curley, a gravel-voiced Irishman. When we first met, he told me that he didn't like "trained seals," as he called all writers who were not reporters. He mentioned several good playwrights and novelists who in past times had been reporters for him. He spoke about how wild their copy was and how lacking in facts. He treated me very well, and sometimes when I wrote a "think" piece, he would put it in bold type.

I don't know what the date was, exactly, but after several months of working on the *Journal* I reviewed a trashy movie called *Svengali,* starring John Barrymore. It was written by Ben Hecht and Charles MacArthur, whose work I always had admired—particularly their play *The Front Page.*

Barrymore jumped up and down like a rabid chimpanzee and hypnotized poor Trilby with what appeared to be small light bulbs in his eyes. It was obvious that Hecht and MacArthur thought the whole thing was junk, and they wrote a junk scenario. I chastized these three men for having lowered their standards to engage in this kind of drivel. The day after this review appeared in the *Journal,* Bill Curley received a telegram which he gave me. It said: "Your column is discontinued. You forget you are working for the masses not the classes. Signed: Widdecombe."

I spent a whole afternoon trying in every way I knew to get Mr. Hearst to answer the phone so I could tell him I wanted him personally to fire me as he personally hired me and I didn't want to be fired by some character named Widdecombe whom I knew naught of.

It turned out that Mr. Barrymore, Mr. MacArthur, and Mr. Hecht were all house guests at San Simeon when my review was printed in the *Journal,* so it was their recommendation that I be discontinued.

THE
ROOSEVELT
YEAR

When I was discontinued by Mr. Widde-combe, I had just set up housekeeping for the first time in my life in one of the better Tonetti houses in Sneden's Land-ing, where I had lived on and off several years before my marriage. (My classmate and the business man-ager of our university comic magazine, *Moonshine*, had married the youngest daughter of Mrs. Marie Tonetti, the widow of a famous sculptor of the time of Stanford White and Rodin. She owned a cluster of cottages strung along the Palisades of the Hudson River in Rockland County and came from a distin-guished line of New York City socialites, her maiden name being Lawrence. Her great uncle was the first mayor of New York City.) It was a blow not only to my pride, but also to my pocketbook, and at a time when my only source of income, *Judge* magazine, was falter-ing and on its way to extinction.

I didn't try to get a job right away, because I was busy with family problems in West Virginia, where the banks were closing one after another. Also, my wife was considering working again in the theatre. But one night in the middle of dinner I was called to the tele-phone by two strangers: Donald Freeman and Clare Boothe Brokaw. They introduced themselves as being coeditors of *Vanity Fair,* and they wished to talk with me about becoming their movie critic.

Besides the satirical articles and the comic use of photographs in the magazine, many distinguished people contributed to *Vanity Fair* while I was em-ployed as the staff movie critic. The other staff people were George Jean Nathan, drama critic; Paul Gallico, sports editor; Steichen, staff photographer; and Covar-rubias, the Mexican artist caricaturist. Among the frequent contributors were Jay Franklin (his real name was John Franklin Carter, and he was to become my superior in the Resettlement Administration two years later when he was the head of the Office of Infor-mation), Julian Huxley, Kay Boyle, John Maynard

Keynes, Ferenc Molnar, Lord Dunsany, J. Frank Dobie, Drew Pearson, Frank Sullivan, Joel Sayer, André Maurois, James M. Cain, John Gunther, Deems Taylor, and others.

Before I had even submitted my first copy, Donald Freeman wrapped himself around a telephone pole up near Rheingold, where he lived, and Clare Boothe Brokaw became managing editor. For all her earned reputation as a malicious if witty commentator, she was a first-class editor and was all business in her editorial offices. But I became slightly uncomfortable with the Condé Nast odor of fashion and chintz bouquets, so I soon arranged to meet my editors at Costello's, a newspaper and writers' bar on Third Avenue frequented by John O'Hara, Ernest Hemingway, and other such rugged individuals.

At that time *Vanity Fair* was undoubtedly the most prestigious magazine in the country. Certainly it was the handsomest: layout, type, photographs, reproductions of paintings. It is a pleasure to look at the old copies of the magazine now compared with what is being published today. I was so impressed with the use of photographs that I began to promote the idea of photographing the great changes that were taking place in America.

Practically all the pictures in my magazine were of people, and some of them were used in a comic manner. I never saw anything of the main streets of little towns with big signs, "Store For Rent," and no shots of rusting coal cars and idle tipples and smokeless smokestacks along the roads I drove on my way back to West Virginia to visit my people.

Shortly after Mr. Roosevelt took office in March 1933, I went about the city trying to get money to make a newsreel of the tragic events that were going on in our country, including the foreclosure on homes and dispossession of farms, the failure of banks, and the migrants from both industry and farms riding the freight trains west.

The only wealthy man who was in the least interested in my idea of a one-hour newsreel of what was going on in America was John Hay Whitney, but being a Republican, he didn't want to invest in a newsreel about Mr. Roosevelt's New Deal.

He did, however, ask if I'd be interested in working on the movie based on *Green Mansions* starring Dolores Del Rio, but I didn't have much excitement about going down to Uruguay and photographing Miss Del Rio, pretty as she was, in a tree full of birds. So I decided if I couldn't make a movie, I would collect news photographs and do a picture book in the form of a newsreel with large captions at the top and concise news paragraphs alongside the big pictures.

Miss Brokaw introduced me to the Condé Nast typographer, whose name was Dr. Agha. He was a passionate admirer of Franklin D. Roosevelt and promptly volunteered to lay out my book and to do it for free. His distinction was such that my publishers, Funk and Wagnalls, didn't object to his taking over that job.

Within a few weeks I finished *The Roosevelt Year,* as my picture book was called, and sold it to Funk and Wagnalls. It was one of the hardest work sessions of my life and one of the coldest. I had rented a little studio apartment on Fifty-sixth Street and Seventh Avenue, and one afternoon in March 1934, just when I was about finished with the book, I went down to the street to buy a newspaper and forgot to put on my jacket. I looked at the headlines, which said it was seventeen degrees below zero and I pretty near froze to death before I got back upstairs.

One morning just before dawn and before I even had a cup of coffee, I was summoned to the telephone by Frank Crowninshield. He had been for many years editor of *Vanity Fair,* but with the coming of Freeman and Brokaw, he had presumably been retired and had been living in Palm Beach. I don't know when he was returned to the editor's desk. He was known to my elders as a bon vivant and bachelor-about-town, but to those who knew him intimately, he was more of a hustler than he was a bon vivant. He was the type of man who favored the company of types with bank accounts such as Nelson Rockefeller. What he had to say that morning was this: "I've been called by Nelson Rockefeller, and he tells me there are people standing in line trying to get into Radio City Music Hall. He also says he doesn't like what you wrote about the opening of the Music Hall, and he doesn't think you belong on *Vanity Fair.* I am sorry to say I agree with him."

I replied immediately in a loud voice that I was delighted Nelson Aldrich Rockefeller had people standing in line trying to get into his big hall but that I thought *Vanity Fair* was supposed to be "The Kaleidoscope Review of the Arts" and that, therefore, we didn't cater to mobs of people standing in line.

It was a blow to have been discontinued from such a prestigious magazine as *Vanity Fair,* and I felt outraged at the man who did it and the way he did it. Condé Nast made a bad decision anyway, because in a few weeks he dismissed Miss Brokaw as managing editor, and then in a little over a year he discontinued the magazine itself. In fact, the last issue of *Vanity Fair* was published in February 1936, having been in existence continuously since January 1914.

As for their discontinued movie critic, his first motion picture, *The Plow That Broke the Plains*, opened at the Rialto Theatre, Forty-second Street and Broadway in New York City, on May 28, 1936, just three months after the death of the magazine.

: : :

Not long after I was fired from *Vanity Fair* at the request of Nelson Aldrich Rockefeller, I was called by Harry Bull, the editor of *Town and Country*, a magazine somewhat like *Vanity Fair* except that it had very few staff writers and very little written material of any kind. The *"Town"* part was mainly interiors of multimillion-dollar residences in New York City where fashionable occasions were reported and photographed. The *"Country"* part was, for the most part, polo matches, tennis, croquet, and yacht races.

I no longer wrote alongside distinguished authors, but I did once again have a handsome publication in which to present my movie writings. Out of sentiment, I also stayed on at *Judge* magazine until it went into receivership and could not pay any writers. I took stock certificates instead of wages from *Judge* in those last days.

One day a university classmate and former business manager of the college comic magazine *West Virginia Moonshine* called me to say that he had gone to work for a new news magazine, and he suggested that I come over to his office and he would take me to meet the managing editor and maybe I could get a job. The next day Jack Ratcliff took me to meet the national affairs editor of *Newsweek*. He was a tall, melancholy fellow named Sam Williamson, and he had been hired away from the *New York Times* to become the editor of the national affairs section of the new magazine. Williamson was a courteous fellow, but he had one disconcerting ailment. Come press day, he would have a bloody nose, and I had to present my final copy to him for approval as he lay full length on his office couch and dabbled with the medication laid out on a side table.

One day I was called by Joe Connelly. Without ever mentioning the *New York Evening Journal*, he said that he had a new job for me. He explained that Colonel Lindberg had visited William Randolph Hearst and told him that the Franklin D. Roosevelt Washington was full of spies. What he, Joe Connelly, wanted me to do was to go to Washington and write about spies.

I told Joe I didn't know anything about Washington to begin with and that I didn't know any spies either, but because of the money and because I was bored with being a rewrite man at *Newsweek* and because I was excited about the New Deal, I took over the job of writing the daily column, "The Washington Side Show." My offices were to be in the *Times Herald,* and the column would be distributed by Universal Services, which was owned by King Features, of which Joe Connelly was the boss.

I asked immediately for expenses and for a female assistant to be my social secretary. My requests were agreed upon, and I left *Newsweek* and approached my new job in Washington with some anxiety, as I had no idea of where to start looking for a spy.

Hearst had had about six or seven men writing "The Washington Side Show," including a good sportswriter named Jim Cannon, so it wasn't a very secure spot for a reporter, but it certainly was a great time, and it proved for me a great opportunity to observe the New Deal firsthand.

Those were exciting days in Washington.

Morris Ernst put me up at the University Club, where I stayed for the first few weeks of my employment. Then I moved over to the Carlton Hotel, where I stayed weekdays, commuting home to Sneden's Landing for the weekends. Traveling to and from Washington on the old Congressional Limited was always a convivial event, as you were sure to know some of the passengers. By the time you had absorbed enough bourbon or scotch to take on your steak and baked potato dinner, you were friends with your neighbors whether you had known them before or not.

The very first thing I did was to set out to find at least one spy. And I did.

I had read the Pearson-Allen column "The Washington Merry-Go-Round" in whatever newspaper it was printed in New York City and enjoyed it very much for its irreverence and impudence. Taking a chance, I wrote to Drew Pearson in Washington and told him I was going to be writing my column (which undoubtedly had been started by the Hearst organization as a rival to "The Washington Merry-Go-Round") and that I would enjoy meeting and talking with him.

He agreed readily and told me to call him when I got to town, which I did. He then told me that there was a strange type of fellow who lived at the Wardman Park Hotel who went horseback riding in Rock Creek Park regularly and that his only source of income seemed to be a check that was sent to the hotel itself once a month with instructions that it be used for the expenses of the mysterious gentleman.

Drew further informed me that the fellow had a girl who was infatuated with him and that the girl was the daughter of an American ambassador to one of the Latin American countries. He related these facts to me at the Troika, a fashionable tavern patronized by politicians and ranking civil servants. While we were talking, he suddenly spied a group of men being

Pare Lorentz, taken on the rooftop of the Department of Agriculture building in Washington, D.C., in the summer of 1936, by Dorothea Lange.

escorted to their tables, and he nudged me and said: "There come two officers of the U.S. Navy League and two diplomats, one from Paraguay and the other from Uruguay."

I forget how many columns I wrote about spies and sinister foreigners in Washington, but so many exciting things were happening that I didn't continue to peek around for mysterious agents.

Among the first events that I recall as being of national importance were the second march on Washington by a veterans' bonus army and U.S. recognition of the Soviet Union. The first veterans' march had been evicted from the district by U.S. troops led by General Douglas MacArthur and his aide, Major Dwight D. Eisenhower, both of whom had changed to dress uniforms in the men's latrine of the Willard Hotel before they took command of the veteran-chasing troops. The second time, President Roosevelt ordered the chief of police of the district, who had been a ranking officer in the First World War, to set up a tent encampment; asked Surgeon General Parran to provide health services, shelter, and food to the veterans; and promised some action for them.

The second event was when, without warning to the State Department or to the press, for that matter, the president suddenly declared that we were going to recognize Communist Russia. Rockets went up in all the press, but I was fortunate. Joe Connelly had sent me, as social secretary, a tall, lanky, sandy-haired reporter who had worked on the *New York Evening Journal.* Her name was Mildred Gilman. (Mildred had recently written a novel, called *Sob Sister,* based on her career, and she had sold it to the movies for a good sum. At some point during her journalistic career she had worked as Heywood Broun's secretary.) When she first reported for duty, I asked her to join me in a slight ramble through the new bars in the district. Repeal had been in existence nationally, but there were provisions that local communities could avoid certain rules, and the district had its own hypocritical regulations.

All the good hotels had open bars, but under the district restrictions there were screens nonchalantly placed around the bar and bartender so you could not see him mixing drinks.

I had expected someone who knew all about the peerage in Washington, but when we went into the old Willard Hotel and sat down at the bar and saw this bamboo screen hiding the bar itself, she and I were quite amazed. I was further amazed when the waiter asked for our order and my secretary looked him in the eye and growled, "Bring me a double scotch and neat, please."

Mildred made friends with the wife of the new Russian ambassador, who was appointed to Washington before the big recognition day. She helped her shop for clothes for herself and her children, buy bedroom curtains and other such things. As a result, I could walk in and out of the Soviet embassy any time I wanted.

But to me, the National Industrial Recovery Act was the most dramatic event in a very dramatic time. The darnedest characters showed up for the NIRA hearings, which covered every occupation and manufacturing facility one could think of: Western Towboat Hearings, Suspender Makers' Hearings, Near Silk Manufacturers' Hearings, and my favorite one, the Copper Hearings. I stayed in the last one long enough to hear the head of his union calling out loudly enough to be heard clear to the Capitol, "And now I'm going to tell you what you're going to have to do with the copper miners: You're going to work them or feed them or fight them."

One final hearing was with the organizing committee of the United Auto Workers, and the heads of the major automobile companies were invited to have a session presided over by Senator Robert F. Wagner of New York. His labor bill had not yet passed the Congress, I believe, but it was in the works. The automobile executives sat in the front row. The UAW executives sat in the middle row. We, the press, sat in the last row. In comes Senator Wagner, and all the union men stood up. They didn't applaud or cheer; they just stood up in recognition of the senator's good deeds. The minute the senator started to speak, all the automobile executives stood up and then walked out of the room.

The senator was visibly hurt, so he ended the meeting with a few kind words of good luck to the union men, and after they left, I spent several minutes with him. He was shaken as well as sad. He finally said: "There's no way to persuade them and no way to change them and it's going to be a long, hard fight."

My book *The Roosevelt Year* came out while I was writing my column in Washington in 1934 and was very well received by political and historical writers. Armed with it, I went to see James Le Cron, who was the private and personal secretary to Henry Wallace. I gave him a copy and left the seed of my idea about photographing the changes in America, such as Tennessee Valley Authority, that were presumably going to take place with the New Deal.

I have no recollection of the date, but the year was 1934, and it was shortly after the anniversary of Mr. Roosevelt's inauguration in March 1933. I wrote a sincere and brief portrait of each of Mr. Roosevelt's cabinet officers and ended remarking that although he seemed a dour sort of Scot, I felt Henry A. Wallace would turn out to be the strongest member of the president's cabinet.

The day after my column about the cabinet appeared in print, in the middle of a beautiful spring afternoon, here comes the wire, BANG!, addressed to the editor of Universal Services. Same fellow. "Discontinue Lorentz immediately. Chief says Henry Wallace is crazy. Signed: Widdecombe."

It took me some time to get over this shock, but in a way I was pleased, because I was not cut out to be either a gossip columnist or a political reporter. Joe Connelly was genuinely dismayed. He called me and said, "Why did you have to be serious? You're supposed to keep on being funny!"

But the seed I had planted with Jim Le Cron started to sprout after I was fired by Brother Widdecombe on behalf of Mr. Hearst. Jim was a neighbor of Henry Wallace and his family in Des Moines, and he was a neighbor now in Washington. I had met him in Des Moines. He married the oldest daughter of Mr. Gardner Cowles, the owner and publisher of the *Des Moines Register Tribune* and the founder of the Cowles Communications empire. My wife's oldest sister had married John Cowles, so we had a connection.

In time Jim agreed with my concept to photograph America, and he introduced me to Secretary Wallace one day in the spring of 1935. The secretary said that the Agricultural Department was an old, old establishment and very set in its ways and would probably not be a good place for me to try to work. He mentioned, however, a brand new organization called the Resettlement Administration. The administrator's name was Dr. Rexford Guy Tugwell, and Secretary Wallace said he would make sure I could go to Tugwell and talk over my plans. By great good fortune, the chief of the Office of Information of this new government organization was John Franklin Carter, who, as I mentioned earlier, wrote for *Vanity Fair* under the name of Jay Franklin. (He also wrote mystery novels under that name.) Carter and I became immediate friends, partly because we had read each other in *Vanity Fair* and liked each other's work. He in turn introduced me to Rex Tugwell. Tugwell also was undersecretary of agriculture. Prior to his

Migrants on the march—baked out and blown out, this family seeks a new home in the West. Scene from The Plow That Broke the Plains.

appointment he had been one of the brain trust from Columbia University, where he was a professor of economics.

Tugwell was so enthusiastic that he suggested that we make eighteen movies. I never did figure out why the number eighteen. Anyway, I thought we'd better make one first and see how it went before we scheduled more. He agreed and asked about a subject. I suggested the Dust Bowl, because I remembered the great vast landscape from my first trip in 1924, particularly the huge arc of sky. I also remembered one day in New York when I was working at *Newsweek* and a heavy, slow-moving, gray cloud, dust from the drought-stricken Great Plains, blew down in the middle of Manhattan Island and settled like an old blanket over the tower of the *New York Times* building at Times Square.

I was assigned to the story, rewriting copy about the Mississippi River's being so low that the blacks along its Southern shores were having religious revival meetings on its banks and about cattlemen grazing their stock on the right-of-ways of railroads because there was forage growing between the ties. The summer before, I had driven with my wife in a secondhand Chevrolet to visit her relatives in Des Moines and Detroit. That was the first time I ever saw heavy farm equipment working at night with the use of big headlights because it was just too hot during the day to work in the fields. Eventually that scene became a part of *The Plow That Broke the Plains*.

In Detroit there was a real deep fear of violence expressed by the well-to-do people, and many of them had installed bulletproof glass in their limousines. There were more than 150,000 unemployed workers lounging around Belle Isle, and most of them were World War I veterans; all those men came from my part of the country: West Virginia, Kentucky, Tennessee, and North Carolina.

I listened to speeches one afternoon, and whether they were religious or fascist or communist or socialist, as I watched the men in the crowds, not any of them seemed to be interested. What they wanted was work, not philosophy.

These experiences—the memory of the sky, rewriting news stories from the drought country, driving through that stricken land, seeing the unemployed at Belle Isle, and noticing the two most prevalent objects in pawn shop windows as I walked down Woodward Avenue in Detroit—guitars and calipers—made a lasting impression and led me to recommend the Dust Bowl to Tugwell as the first subject we should dramatize in our first movie.

I was employed as a consultant to come down from New York two or three days a week at a salary of $18.06 a day and $6.00 per diem for board and lodging to explain my craft to my superiors. My classification was technical consultant. By the time I employed cameramen, narrator, and my composer, Virgil Thomson, we all were classified as being worth $25.00 a day.

The problems of introducing a new idea to the bureaucracy of government are all set forth comprehensively and clearly by Professor Robert L. Snyder in *Pare Lorentz and the Documentary Film* (University of Oklahoma Press, 1968), so I will not repeat the incidents and the aggravations here.

THE

MAKING

OF *THE*

PLOW

THAT

BROKE

THE

PLAINS

One year shy of a half-century I received a letter from my natal town of Clarksburg, West Virginia, which not only was a pleasant one but which included a report about the reaction of the students in the local grade school after they had witnessed *The Plow That Broke the Plains* and *The River*: "The students felt that these documentaries were easier to understand than contemporary documentaries because of the use of more footage and less dialogue." After all these years it is fortifying to realize that my original concept of using pictures, music, and words still is correct.

By the time I had finally cut the footage of *The Plow That Broke the Plains* down to the running time of Virgil Thomson's full-length score, which was approximately thirty minutes, and by the time I had arranged for a recording of that score, I suddenly realized that I did not have any words written for a narration.

From the beginning of my moviemaking years, even though I had never set foot in the cutting room or been behind a camera, I wished to keep control of the three elements of my film—pictures, music, and words—and to emphasize the elements in that order.

For example, Alexander Smallens did not conduct the chairs of the New York Philharmonic to *film*, as is the custom in Hollywood. The musicians were recording a concert, and when we hit midnight, I recall with some emotion, I told Alex that I simply did not have any money to go on. Because the musicians were members of Local 802, if we had gone on past midnight, officially they would have been on "golden hours," or triple time.

Anyway, Smallens banged his baton and said beseechingly to the orchestra, particularly the fiddle section, that they were playing new music by Virgil Thomson, and he would like them to record the last sequence again, which they then did several times on their own time. Because Alex asked their permission,

Scene by the Camp at Bakersfield, California. From The Plow That Broke the Plains.

they did not charge the union triple time—not *any* time—for that extra hour of recording.

When finally I had written the words for *The Plow That Broke the Plains*, I asked Thomas Hardie Chalmers to narrate them for me. Typically he bellowed—and he could really bellow, having been a Metropolitan Opera Company singer—"I hate narrators." I explained that I did, too, and that's why I had asked him to work for me. I did not, however, because of his great voice and forceful personality, let him see the film before he narrated my words.

I did play the recording of Virgil's music for him. I had asked Virgil to orchestrate his score so that where I needed words—yet unwritten—I would not have to ask the sound man to pull down volume periodically to allow for the narration, so Virgil diminished the sound either by limiting the musicians or by using woodwinds instead of horns, etc.

A cut movie and a matching full-length score—but no words.

After days of running the sound and pictures with my editor, Leo Zochling, I became almost desperate about what to say and how to say it. A theatrical producer who was a neighbor helped me with the problem by asking, "Who's talking?"

Later, still puzzled, I spent a weekend with old friends, Dan and

Camera crew at railroad crossing outside Bakersfield, California, waiting for migrants to cross the tracks in their jalopies, October 1935. Left to right: Pare Lorentz, Paul Ivano, and assistant cameraman (behind camera).

Peggy Lindley, at Dan's father-in-law's home at Black Point. My hostess had put Saint-Exupéry's book *Night Flight* on my bedside table. Besides enjoying it, suddenly the design of the book hit me as being appropriate to my needs. Beginning with the second chapter, the opening words of the chapters were printed separately on a blank page prior to turning to the chapter itself. For example, under the heading of

Dust around a ranch house, Texas Panhandle, October 1937. From The Plow That Broke the Plains.

chapter 3 we read, "THE SOUND OF THE DISTANT ENGINE SWELLED AND THICKENED." Turning the page to the chapter proper, we see the line repeated: "The sound of the distant engine swelled and thickened." I felt that by this device the author had attempted to create a rhythm of propeller blades and the feeling of flight. Whatever that great Frenchman's intent, I did then resolve to use a minimum of words and to reiterate them in rhythm with the music wherever possible.

Another work probably influenced my writing. Clear back in 1927 I had reviewed F. W. Murnau's *Sunrise*. It was a sound-on-film movie, inasmuch as it had a symphonic musical score. There were, however, no spoken words. I recall that the printed captions were either reiterated or repeated. For example: "The woman from the city. The woman from the city." Either as captions or as reiterative captions, they were impressive the way they were placed, with the music helping to create the moods.

I asked the agricultural experts in the Resettlement Administration to supply me with the basic statistics which are in the narration, starting with the Prologue showing a map of the Great Plains and the amount of acreage and ending with the number of displaced and blown-out farmers on the road at that time.

In an article in *U.S. Camera* I gave credit to Dorothea Lange for a few of the lines in my narration which were taken from the captions of the migrants she photographed. Two of them are spoken over the last sequence in which the migrants unload outside of the tent camp at Bakersfield, California: "Blown out, baked out and broke," and "No place to go . . . and no place to stop."

My intent almost a half-century ago was to have the pictures tell their story; to augment that story with music that would not only be an accompaniment but also would evoke emotions related to the lives of the people concerned, and finally to write the fewest possible words, solely for explanation and clarity, and to have them as much as possible in time with the music.

According to the wonderful grade school children in the Towers Elementary School in Clarksburg, West Virginia, evidently that design of fifty years ago still works.

THE

Written and directed by Pare Lorentz

PLOW

Photographers: Ralph Steiner, Paul Strand,
Leo Hurwitz, Paul Ivano

THAT

BROKE

Film Editor: Leo Zochling

THE

Music by Virgil Thomson

PLAINS

Conductor: Alexander Smallens

Narrator: Thomas Chalmers

Produced by the Office of Information
Resettlement Administration
John Franklin Carter, Director

I : PROLOGUE

This is a record of land . . .
of soil, rather than people—
a story of the Great Plains:
the 400,000 acres of
wind-swept grass lands that spread up
from the Texas Panhandle to Canada . . .
A high, treeless continent,
without rivers, without streams . . .
A country of high winds, and sun . . .
and of little rain . . .

II : GRASS

The grass lands . . .
a treeless wind-swept continent of grass
stretching from the broad Texas Panhandle
up to the mountain reaches of Montana
and to the Canadian border.
A country of high winds and sun . . .

III : CATTLE

First came the cattle . . .
an unfenced range a thousand miles long . . .
an uncharted ocean of grass,
the southern range for winter grazing
and the mountain plateaus for summer.
It was a cattleman's Paradise.
Up from the Rio Grande . . .
in from the rolling prairies . . .
down clear from the eastern highways
the cattle rolled into the old buffalo range.
For a decade the world discovered the grasslands
and poured cattle into the plains.
The railroads brought markets to the edge of

Scene from the cattle sequence in The Plow That Broke the Plains.

Outside Dalhart, Texas, October 1935. From The Plow That Broke the Plains.

the plains . . .
land syndicates sprang up overnight
and the cattle rolled into the West.

IV : HOMESTEADER

But the railroad brought the world into the plains
. . . new populations, new needs crowded
the last frontier.
Once again the plowman followed the herds
and the pioneer came to the plains.
Make way for the plowman!
High winds and sun . . .
High winds and sun . . .
a country without rivers and with little rain.
Settler, plow at your peril!

V : WARNING

Many were disappointed.
The rains failed . . .
and the sun baked the light soil.
Many left . . . they fought the loneliness
and the hard years . . .
But the rains failed them.

VI : WAR

Many were disappointed, but the great day
was coming . . . the day of new causes—
new profits—new hopes.
"Wheat will win the war!"
"Plant wheat . . ."
"Plant the cattle ranges . . ."
"Plant your vacant lots . . . plant wheat!"
"Wheat for the boys over there!"

"Wheat for the Allies!"
"Wheat for the British!"
"Wheat for the Belgians!"
"Wheat for the French!"
"Wheat at any price . . ."
"Wheat will win the war!"

VII : BLUES

Then we reaped the golden harvest . . .
then we really plowed the plains . . .
we turned under millions of new acres for war.
We had the man-power . . .
we invented new machinery . . .
the world was our market.
By 1933 the old grass lands had become the new
wheat lands . . . a hundred million acres . . .
two hundred million acres . . .
More wheat!

VIII : DROUGHT

A country without rivers . . . without streams . . .
with little rain . . .
Once again the rains held off and the
sun baked the earth.
This time no grass held moisture against the
winds and sun . . . this time millions of acres
of plowed land lay open to the sun.

IX : DEVASTATION

Baked out—blown out—and broke!
Year in, year out, uncomplaining they fought
the worst drought in history . . .
their stock choked to death on the barren land . . .

Dust storm approaching Texas Panhandle, 1935.

Evicted by drought—a family leaving its home in the plains. From The Plow That Broke the Plains.

their homes were nightmares of swirling dust
night and day.
Many were ahead of it—but many stayed
until stock, machinery, homes, credit, food,
and even hope were gone.
On to the West!
Once again they headed into the setting sun . . .
Once again they headed West out of
the Great Plains and hit the highways
for the Pacific Coast, the last border.
Blown out—baked out—and broke . . .
nothing to stay for . . . nothing to hope for . . .
homeless, penniless and bewildered they joined
the great army of the highways.
No place to go . . . and no place to stop.
Nothing to eat . . . nothing to do . . .
their homes on four wheels . . . their work a
desperate gamble for a day's labor in the fields
along the highways. . . .
The price of a sack of beans or a tank of gas . . .
All they ask is a chance to start over . . .
And a chance for their children to eat,
to have medical care, to have homes again.
50,000 a month! . . .
The sun and winds wrote the most tragic chapter
in American agriculture.

THE MAKING OF *THE* RIVER

I know he was wearing striped pants and a cutaway, and I'm sure it was the occasion of the funeral of Louis Howe. I had come to see my boss, Rexford Guy Tugwell, head of the Resettlement Administration, in order to tell him I was resigning and going back to New York to concentrate on writing. I noted that we had achieved our objective—we had made a motion picture about a national problem in which he was involved and it was of such merit that it had been given high critical acclaim and award mentions and had been exhibited in thousands of commercial movie theaters.

He spoke of the bereavement of President Roosevelt and how Louis Howe had dedicated his life to the president and in turn had become one of his dearest friends as well as his confidential advisor.

As I was turning to leave his office, I saw a framed profile map of the Mississippi River valley on the wall. I turned to him and said that if he was ever going to make another movie, this river valley would be an obvious and wonderful subject. He immediately asked me to sit down and tell him how much such a movie would cost and where to begin. I told him we would start at Lake Itasca and follow a drop of water, in effect, to the Gulf of Mexico. In answer to his question about cost, and having no time to do any figuring, I did some mental calculations and came up with the sum of $50,000. (We came in with the master print at, I believe, $49,500.) Tugwell asked me to wait in his office, and he either telephoned the White House or went over in person, and in about half an hour he returned and said the president had given his approval to the project.

Beginning with that approval, I began to collect information from all the government sources, including the Indian Bureau, the Interior Department, Geological Survey, and so on. (From the Indian Bureau I was given the correct translations and pronunciations of the Indian names of the rivers.)

I had hoped that as work went along I could get enough ahead of the production to work with Virgil Thomson on an oratorio using work songs: lumber, rafting, levee building, railroad tie-laying—the works. Virgil always has said that if I had ever entertained such an idea with him, he would have written an oratorio provided I furnished him with words. I recall playing Honegger's "King David Oratorio" until the record was unplayable, but the picture came first, and as usual I proceeded with the film production.

I later worked with Virgil just as we had done with *The Plow That Broke the Plains,* although I had much less time with him, because of constant money problems. Among other problems, our organization was declared unconstitutional by the Supreme Court, and we were made an adjunct of the Department of Agriculture, which before we had finished editing the films cut off our funds.

But this is about the words of *The River.*

I finished shooting with the camera crew on the lower river around New Orleans in January 1937—so I thought. By the time I reached Washington, it had continually rained for days, and by the middle of the month the huge 1937 flood was under way. I went back down the river and met the crew at Memphis, and we started over. When I came back from having been in the flood area, my great editor at *McCall's,* Otis Wiese, asked me to write a report about the flood. I agreed because it seemed to me a good way to practice my narration for my uncut and unscored movie.

After I had written at least five thousand words, I realized that just to explain the river and then to detail the history and finally to describe the flood, I would be unable to jam such a narration into a thirty-minute motion picture. Having all my research from the various government departments scattered around my work room, I put each section on the floor—rivers, forests, flood reports, erosion, etc.—and one night, nonstop until daybreak, I wrote substantially the words of *The River.*

I took the long, factual account of the river and the flood and the little lyrical piece to my editor. He chose to run the lyrical version as a frontispiece "editorial" in the May 1937 issue of *McCall's* magazine. In February 1938 Otis wrote a very nice sketch of me for his magazine in which he stated that after the words of *The River* were printed in *McCall's,* "It was reprinted in more than 8 million copies of newspapers and magazines."

While I was assembling *The River* in Hollywood with Lloyd Nosler (the film editor King Vidor had recommended to me), my government relations were being bounced around by the Supreme Court and by President Roosevelt. After the Resettlement Administration was adjudged unconstitutional by the court, it was moved by executive order into the Agriculture Department and renamed the Farm Security Administration. My immediate superior and my friend John Franklin Carter resigned as chief of the Office of Information and was employed as a syndicated political commentator by the *Des Moines Register Tribune*, a respected newspaper owned and run by the Cowles family. Rexford Guy Tugwell resigned his post both as administrator of the original Resettlement Administration and as undersecretary of agriculture. He went to Mexico for a brief time to work as an agricultural consultant to President Cardenas. A Rhodes scholar from Texas, John Fischer, was named to take John Carter's place as chief of information for the FSA.

There were times during the months of May and June 1937 when I was assembling with Nosler the more than eighty thousand feet of film we had to deal with that I decided to quit and throw the whole shebang away as far as I was concerned, but every time I did this Nosler would bring out an old tattered issue of the May 1937 issue of *McCall's* with my lyrical words of *The River* and would successfully plead with me to keep working. With the end of the fiscal year in June, I was off the government payroll and still had not been given any complete score by Virgil Thomson. We had quarreled over the steamboat sequence, and Virgil finally said he was going to Paris. My good secretary Miss Roberts called me at my home one day after Virgil had given me this announcement, and I said that there could only be one more thing that could happen to me, and that was to hear that my father had died. That proved to be true, so I had to take time out to take over the problems of my father's affairs, my mother, and my only sister, who had married not long before and was quite pregnant at that time. It was a melancholy week added to my not having a musical score and not having any salary from the U.S. government.

The day after the Fourth of July holiday, my secretary called to say that Virgil Thomson had left a note for me. The note was in the form of a lullaby he had written for my baby son, who had been born February 11. I just made it out of the flood area in time for that event.

Virgil and I agreed on the steamboat sequence finally, and the music was recorded. Tom Chalmers did the narration as he had done *The*

Plow, and I was ready to re-record when my producer, the Resettlement Administration, was renamed, so I had to have Chalmers make a sound track using the new name wherever I had "Resettlement Administration" in the final sequence.

I had asked General Services Studio, with whom I had recorded *The Plow*, to make the sound track of *The River*, with Alex Smallens conducting, but I was not too happy with it. I wished to go to Hollywood for a private showing, hoping for a release from one of the big companies, so I asked them if they would subcontract a re-recording with Samuel Goldwyn Studios, and they agreed to this (with no profit). I was assured that although I was off the payroll, that money for the production of *The River* had been set aside and I still had enough money in my budget to re-record. Even so, I was at a low ebb physically and mentally.

One of the Information Office employees was George Gercke, who had been a *New York World* reporter assigned to Albany when Franklin D. Roosevelt was governor. He had lent a hand during the successful exhibition of *The Plow That Broke the Plains*, and he knew of my frustration. I had completed a thirty-minute film that was deeply praised by my immediate friends to whom I showed it, but I had no idea of how to get a federal government representative to help me show it to potential movie distributors. He suggested that we show it to the president, but Tugwell had resigned by then, I did not know Dr. Will Alexander, his successor, and John Fischer seemed a literary man with slight Republican party tendencies.

One gloomy September day Gercke called me from Washington and said he was going to New York, where he had made arrangements for us to show *The River* to President Roosevelt at Hyde Park. The president was in residence there prior to taking a special train across the continent, the trip being publicized for the purpose of a rededication of the Bonneville Dam and a discussion of Grand Coulee. Actually it also was to be a political trip on which he would make speeches for Democrats who were in trouble for having supported the president in some of his activities. I told Gercke that I didn't see how I could go to a man's house without an invitation, but George convinced me that the arrangement had been made, so we drove up to Hyde Park in a driving equinoctial storm. We were intercepted twice on the way to the front door by security men and the Secret Service, but George talked them into letting us in.

We sat on an outdoor, covered porch decorated with old oil paintings of men-of-war, then we were ushered into the front hall in time to see the door to the dining room open and see the president of the United States wheeling out. He looked at Gercke and said, "George, what are you doing here?"

My heart sank. Uninvited guest. George weakly said, "Mr. President, you remember Pare Lorentz. We came up to show you *The River*."

The president smiled congenially and said, "That's good. I was talking about it at dinner, asking whatever happened to that production."

We were joined by the other guests, including a bevy of Roosevelts and Delanos, as they had been in a horse show and were anxious to look at the newsreels of their events, which were to open the program. Next came the newsreels of Mrs. James Roosevelt, the president's mother, and her entourage during a trip to Europe. There were shots of the Japanese navy shelling someplace, with the result being that the stock market collapsed and the president that day ordered Secretary Morgenthau to return from California, having sent a navy amphibian aircraft for the secretary's use.

After the newsreels, the Delano and Roosevelt visitors all left, as did Mrs. Roosevelt and the president's mother. Eleanor Roosevelt came over to George and me and apologized for leaving, as she had to correct the galley proofs of her autobiography. That left the help, the projection crew, James Roosevelt's wife, Betsy Cushing, George and myself, and, of course, the president. We were taken aback when instead of *The River* we were treated to a showing of the full-length feature film *Thin Ice*, starring Sonja Henie. It was after midnight when that epic finished and *The River* was put on. The president did not speak one word during the showing, but when it was over, he called to Betsy and said, "Bring Pare down here. I want to talk with him."

I went down and crouched beside his wheelchair. He removed his pince-nez glasses with that well-known flourish and said, "That's a grand movie. What can I do to help?"

George said he could have jumped through a window, and I was so full of things I wanted to say, I blurted out, "Mr. Roosevelt, you can put me back on the payroll, for one thing."

His eyes turned cold, and then in a cold tone he turned to Betsy and said, "Get Tom Corcoran to come down here."

In a short time Corcoran, whom I had not met before, was ordered by the president, who said to him curtly, "I want you to look after this man." He didn't ask me any details but went into the distribution problem by saying, "I think this movie is good enough for chain theatres." He brought up various political figures, but I finally said that I had an idea. I then told him that if we opened in New York City, the Yale news types on *Time* magazine and suburban types on the newspapers would be condescending if not denigrating toward the South in their movie reviews.

I wanted to go to New Orleans, and if the river scholars and historians liked the movie, we could keep going up the river to Memphis, Saint Louis, and so on. "It's a grand idea," the president said, and off we went in a driving rain, singing all the way.

I must have had sixteen telephone calls from Washington before noon the next day. Corcoran had started to look after me. Everything about my experience with Goldwyn's Gordon Sawyer and his sound-mate Lanning was a delight. Also was my luncheon with Mr. Goldwyn, which took place in the little backlot commissary. After I thanked Mr. Goldwyn for taking a subcontract to rescore *The River*, he said, "I want you on my lot so I can find out how you make movies." Two old friends from the East, George Haight and Merritt Hulburt (who had been an associate editor on the *Saturday Evening Post*), were young producers for Goldwyn, so it helped pave my way through his chain of employees.

It was not until I got to Chicago on the way to New Orleans that I realized I had no literary or theatrical acquaintances in the city. On the spur of the moment I called their publishers and got the addresses of Roark Bradford, the author of the collection of black stories "Old Man Adam and His Children" which had been made into the prize-winning play *Green Pastures* and later into a movie, and Lyle Saxon, author of a photographic book on New Orleans and a book about the big 1927 flood that took place during Coolidge's presidency. Saxon was also the head of the Works Progress Administration Writers' Project in New Orleans. I wired each man, saying, "I need help. Would appreciate your advice. Meet me at the St. Charles Hotel anytime after ten o'clock tonight."

It turned out Saxon lived at the Saint Charles, and it turned out that Roark Bradford lived at 719 Toulouse Street in the midst of the French Quarter and that his home was a refuge for all visiting artists, writers, playwrights, etc.

I flew to New Orleans from Chicago in a little Lockheed Electra through a ferocious line storm, and we were two hours late. I went straight up to my room, figuring my guests would have left long since, when the phone rang and this guttural voice roared, "Lorentz, you silly so-and-so. We've been sitting down here two hours waiting for you." I joined them immediately, and after one drink, and making sure we all knew something about each other, Brad said, "Why don't we all go over to my house?" which we promptly did not only that night, but also every night up to the opening.

Brad and Lyle collected a group of ladies whom they always used to promote events, and they found an independent theatre owner whom I persuaded to cancel his own bookings for one night and put on a "world premier." He was a tall, lanky Southerner and before he made the final agreement, he said, "If your audience damages my screen, will the government pay for it?"

I said, "What damage?"

"I have another theatre up in Greenville, and when the audience doesn't like the picture, they throw rocks at the screen."

I reassured him on that point, but as he was showing four westerns for ten cents' admission, there was a pretty high fragrance in his theatre, so I bought $750 worth of flowers and had them put in strategic places throughout the theatre and charged them to the U.S. Department of Agriculture. Even after the success of *The River* there was some criticism of my extravagance.

There were many cities where Walt Disney was locked out because he would not agree to the terms of the big chain theatre companies. For that reason he would let me have a print of a new Walt Disney cartoon wherever I previewed *The River*. This time he sent me a print of a short that introduced Pluto, the dog, to the world. Along with that I told my theatre owner that I knew of a fine feature film that was having a problem getting released because it was made in England and Will Hays didn't like his sponsors to have foreign film competition. The film was *The Thirty-nine Steps*, directed by Alfred Hitchcock.

The world premiere of *The River* took place in New Orleans on October 29, 1937, just a little over a month after Mr. Roosevelt had approved the idea. The owner and manager of the Strand Theatre, where the opening was held, sent me the following telegram:

Held world premiere of River October 29th three hundred and fifty leading people at New Orleans. Reaction was wonderful. I personally contacted several hundred of these people after premiere. They congratulated me for being able to bring film of that nature to my screen. Nineteen schools of the city had a representative from their history class to see River. Also showed Rivers [*sic*] to some 20,000 patrons. Audience reaction great. The public needs more history shorts like The River. Hoping Minneapolis enjoys it as New Orleans did.

From beginning to end that was one of the most memorable evenings of my life, and I think two incidents are worth recounting. I had asked Roark Bradford to sit by me, and it wasn't until the movie came on that I realized that he had not seen the picture and had no idea of what it was like. Neither did any of the other guests, for that matter. He made a little taut face as the movie started, but when we came to the levee sequence, he started chuckling, turned to me, and said, "That's a real levee outfit of mules. Look at that old gray mule slacking back in the harness, letting the black mule take all the weight."

Prior to writing my outline of *The River* for my superiors to approve, I had stated that somewhere we had to mention the Civil War. I was met with ferocious denial. It was explained to me this would outrage the Southern congressmen, so we couldn't bring the matter up. In my research I came across two volumes of Major Robert E. Lee, Jr.'s, memoirs of his father. There was a copy of the letter Lee had read to his troops by company commanders as he rode by the men on his horse Traveler. I asked Virgil Thomson to arrange for trumpets to play "Retreat" while this letter rolled slowly on the screen, and I had General Services Studio impose flames over the words as they rolled by. Herewith is General Lee's letter of surrender.

April 10, 1865
After four years of arduous service marked by unsurpassed courage and fortitude, the Army of Northern Virginia has been compelled to yield to overwhelming numbers and resources.

I need not tell the survivors of so many hard-fought battles, who have remained steadfast to the last that I have consented to this result from no distrust of them . . .

But feeling that valor and devotion could accomplish nothing that could compensate for the loss that would have attended the continuation of the contest, I have determined to avoid useless sacrifice of those whose past services have endeared them to their country-men . . .

With an increasing admiration of your constancy and devotion to your country, and a grateful remembrance of your kind and generous consideration of myself, I bid you an affectionate farewell.

R. E. Lee, General

When the scroll rolled to its end and the name Robert E. Lee, General, came on the screen, the entire audience without a signal or a sound came up, and they didn't sit down until Lee's name went off the screen. I never heard a peep about this scroll from anybody in the government, much less the Agriculture Department.

: : :

The River opened in New York City at the Criterion Theatre on February 4, 1938, and received extraordinary praise from all New York critics and from literary and dramatic critics as well.

Subsequent to the successful opening in New York City, Paramount Pictures took over chain theatre distribution of the movie, and shortly after that happened, Bill Soskin, editor of Stackpole Sons Publishers, said he wanted to bring out *The River* as a picture textbook, which he did. He presented me with two beautifully bound special limited editions of *The River*—the first for me and the second for the president of the United States.

Over the years some parts of my narration of *The River* have appeared in various anthologies, including *The Pocket Companion*, published by Pocketbooks in 1942, and *A New Anthology of Modern Poetry* by Selden Rodman, published by Random House in 1938.

Over the years the motion picture has received several awards and citations. *The River* received the award for the best documentary film by the International Film Festival in Venice in August 1938.

THE

RIVER

Written and directed by Pare Lorentz

Photographers: Stacy Woodard, Floyd Crosby, Willard Van Dyke

Editors: Leo Zochling, Lloyd Nosler

Music by Virgil Thomson

Narrator: Thomas Chalmers

From as far East as New York,
    Down from the turkey ridges of the Alleghenies
Down from Minnesota, twenty five hundred miles,
    The Mississippi River runs to the Gulf.
Carrying every drop of water, that flows down
    two-thirds the continent.
Carrying every brook and rill, rivulet and creek,
Carrying all the rivers that run down two-thirds
    the continent,
The Mississippi runs to the Gulf of Mexico.

Down the Yellowstone, the Milk, the White and
    Cheyenne;
The Cannonball, the Musselshell, the James and
    the Sioux;
Down the Judith, the Grand, the Osage, and the
    Platte,
The Skunk, the Salt, the Black and Minnesota;
Down the Rock, the Illinois, and the Kankakee
The Allegheny, the Monongahela, Kanawha, and
    Muskingum;
Down the Miami, the Wabash, the Licking and
    the Green
The Cumberland, the Kentucky, and the Tennessee;
Down the Ouachita, the Wichita, the Red, and Yazoo.

Down the Missouri three thousand miles from the
    Rockies;
Down the Ohio a thousand miles from the Alle-
    ghenies;
Down the Arkansas fifteen hundred miles from
    the Great Divide;
Down the Red, a thousand miles from Texas;
Down the great Valley, twenty-five hundred miles
    from Minnesota,
Carrying every rivulet and brook, creek and rill,
Carrying all the rivers that run down two-thirds
    the continent—
The Mississippi runs to the Gulf.

Site of Hiwassee Dam, North Carolina mountains. From opening sequence, The River.

New Orleans to Baton Rouge,
Baton Rouge to Natchez,
Natchez to Vicksburg,
Vicksburg to Memphis,
Memphis to Cairo—
We built a dyke a thousand miles long.
Men and mules, mules and mud;
Mules and mud a thousand miles up the
    Mississippi.
A century before we bought the great Western
    River, the Spanish and the French built
    dykes to keep the Mississippi out of New
    Orleans at flood stage.

In forty years we continued the levee the entire
    length of the great alluvial Delta,
That mud plain that extends from the Gulf of
    Mexico clear to the mouth of the Ohio.

Cotton loading, Anderson-Clayton Company, New Orleans, January 1937. From The River.

The ancient valley built up for centuries by the
   old river spilling her floods across the bottom
   of the continent—
A mud delta of forty thousand square miles.
Men and mules, mules and mud—
New Orleans to Baton Rouge,
Natchez to Vicksburg,
Memphis to Cairo—
A thousand miles up the river.

We rolled a million bales down the river for
   Liverpool and Leeds . . .

1860: we rolled four million bales down the river;

Rolled them off Alabama,

Rolled them off Mississippi,

Rolled them off Louisiana,

Rolled them down the river!

We fought a war.

We fought a war and kept the west bank
of the river free of slavery forever.

But we left the old South impoverished
and stricken.

Doubly stricken, because, beyond the tragedy
of war, already the frenzied cotton culti-
vation of a quarter of a century had taken
toll of the land.

We mined the soil for cotton until it would
yield no more, and then moved west.

We fought a war, but there was a double
tragedy—the tragedy of land twice
impoverished.

Black spruce and Norway pine,
Douglas fir and Red cedar,
Scarlet oak and Shagbark hickory,
Hemlock and aspen—
There was lumber in the North.

The war impoverished the old South, the railroads
killed the steamboats.
But there was lumber in the North.
Heads up!
Lumber on the upper river.

Heads up!
Lumber enough to cover all Europe.
Down from Minnesota and Wisconsin.
Down to St. Paul;
Down to St. Louis and St. Joe—

Erosion, southern Mississippi, November 1936. From The River.

Lumber for the new continent of the West.
Lumber for the new mills.

There was lumber in the North
    and coal in the hills.
Iron and coal down the Monongahela.
Iron and coal down the Allegheny.
Iron and coal down the Ohio.
Down to Pittsburgh,
Down to Wheeling,
Iron and coal for the steel mills,
    for the railroad driving
West and South, for the new cities
    of the Great Valley—

We built new machinery and cleared new
    land in the West.

Ten million bales down to the Gulf—

Cotton for the spools of England and France.

Fifteen million bales down to the Gulf—

Cotton for the spools of Italy and Germany.

We built a hundred cities and a thousand towns;
St. Paul and Minneapolis,
Davenport and Keokuk,
Moline and Quincy,
Cincinnati and St. Louis,
Omaha and Kansas City . . .
Across to the Rockies and down from Minnesota,
Twenty-five hundred miles to New Orleans,
We built a new continent.

Black spruce and Norway pine,
Douglas fir and Red cedar,
Scarlet oak and Shagbark hickory.
We built a hundred cities and a thousand towns—
But at what a cost!
We cut the top off Minnesota and sent it down the
    river.
We cut the top off Wisconsin and sent it down the
    river.
We left the mountains and the hills slashed and
    burned,
And moved on.

The water comes downhill, spring and fall;
Down from the cut-over mountains,
Down from the plowed-off slopes,
Down every brook and rill, rivulet and creek,
Carrying every drop of water that flows down
    two-thirds the continent
1903 and 1907,
1913 and 1922,
1927,

Flood on the lower Mississippi River, February 1937. From The River.

1936,
1937!

Down from Pennsylvania and Ohio,
Kentucky and West Virginia,
Missouri and Illinois,
Down from North Carolina and Tennessee—
Down the Judith, the Grand, the Osage, and the
    Platte,
The Rock, the Salt, the Black and Minnesota,
Down the Monongahela, the Allegheny, Kanawha
    and Muskingum,
The Miami, the Wabash, the Licking and the
    Green,
Down the White, the Wolfe, and the Cache,
Down the Kaw and Kaskaskia, the Red and Yazoo,
Down the Cumberland, Kentucky and the
    Tennessee—

Escape from flood on the Mississippi, February 1937. From The River.

Down to the Mississippi.
New Orleans to Baton Rouge—
Baton Rouge to Natchez—
Natchez to Vicksburg—
Vicksburg to Memphis—
Memphis to Cairo—
A thousand miles down the levee the long vigil
   starts.
Thirty-eight feet at
   Baton Rouge
River rising.
Helena: river rising.
Memphis: river rising.
Cairo: river rising.
A thousand miles to go,
A thousand miles of levee to hold—

Coastguard patrol needed at Paducah!
Coastguard patrol needed at Paducah!

200 boats—wanted at Hickman!
200 boats—wanted at Hickman!

Levee patrol: men to Blytheville!
Levee patrol: men to Blytheville!

2000 men wanted at Cairo!
2000 men wanted at Cairo!

A hundred thousand men to fight the old river.

We sent armies down the river to help the
    engineers fight a battle on a two thousand
    mile front:
The Army and the Navy,
The Coast Guard and the Marine Corps,
the CCC and the WPA
The Red Cross and the Health Service
They fought night and day to hold the old river
    off the valley.
Food and water needed at Louisville: 500 dead,
    5000 ill;
Food and water needed at Cincinnati;
Food and water and shelter and clothing
    needed for 750,000 flood victims;

Food and medicine needed at Lawrenceburg;

35,000 homeless in Evansville;

Food and medicine needed in Aurora;

Food and medicine and shelter and clothing
    for 750,000 down in the valley.

Last time we held the levees,
But the old river claimed her valley.
She backed into Tennessee and Arkansas
And Missouri and Illinois.
She left stock drowned, houses torn loose,
Farms ruined.

An abandoned East Tennessee farm. From The River.

1903 and 1907.
1913 and 1922.
1927.
1936.
1937!

We built a hundred cities and a
    thousand towns—
But at what a cost!

Spring and fall the water comes down, and for
    years the old river has taken a toll from the
    Valley more terrible than ever she does in
    flood times.
Year in, year out, the water comes down
From a thousand hillsides, washing the top off
    the Valley.
For fifty years we dug for cotton and moved West

Eroded hillside outside Jackson, Mississippi, November 1937. From The River.

    when the land gave out.
For fifty years we plowed for corn, and moved on
    when the land gave out.
Corn and wheat; wheat and cotton—we planted
    and plowed with no thought for the future—
And four hundred million tons of top soil,
Four hundred million tons of our most valuable
    natural resource have been washed into the
    Gulf of Mexico every year.

And poor land makes poor people.
Poor people make poor land.
For a quarter of a century we have been forcing
    more and more farmers into tenancy.
Today forty percent of all the farmers in the great
    Valley are tenants.

Ten percent are share croppers,
Down on their knees in the valley,
A share of the crop their only security,
No home, no land of their own,

Rescue camp, Camden, Arkansas, January 1937. From The River.

Aimless, footloose, and impoverished,
Unable to eat even from the land because their
   cash crop is their only livelihood.

Credit at the store is their only reserve.

And a generation growing up with no new
   land in the West—

A generation whose people knew
   King's Mountain and Shiloh;

A generation whose people knew
   Fremont and Custer;

But a generation facing a life of dirt
   and poverty,

Eroded land outside Jackson, Mississippi, November 1937. From The River.

Disease and drudgery;

Growing up without proper food,
    medical care or schooling,

"Ill-clad, ill-housed, and ill-fed"—

And in the greatest river valley in the world.

EPILOGUE

There is no such thing as an ideal river in Nature,
    but the Mississippi is out of joint.
Dust blowing in the West—floods raging in the East—
We have seen these problems growing to horrible extremes.

When first we found the great valley it was forty
    percent forested.

Today, for every hundred acres of forests we found,
we have ten left.
Today five percent of the entire valley is ruined forever
by agricultural use!
Twenty-five percent of the topsoil has been shoved by
the old river into the Gulf of Mexico.
Today two out of five farmers in the valley are tenant
farmers—ten percent of them share croppers, living
in a state of squalor unknown to the poorest
peasant in Europe.
And we are forcing thirty-thousand more into tenancy
and cropping every year.
Flood control of the Mississippi means control in the great
Delta that must carry all the water brought down from
two-thirds the continent
And control of the Delta means control of the little rivers,
the great arms running down from the uplands. And
the old river can be controlled.
We had the power to take the valley apart—we have
the power to put it together again.

In 1933 we started, down on the Tennessee
River, when our Congress created the Tennessee
Valley Authority, commissioned to develop navigation, flood control, agriculture, and industry
in the valley: a valley that carries more rain
fall than any other in the country; the valley
through which the Tennessee used to roar down to
Paducah in flood times with more water than any
other tributary of the Ohio.

First came the dams.

Up on the Clinch, at the head of the river, we
built Norris Dam, a great barrier to hold water
in flood times and to release water down the river
for navigation in low water season.

Next came Wheeler, first in a series of great
barriers that will transform the old Tennessee
into a link of fresh water pools locked and
dammed, regulated and controlled, down six
hundred fifty miles to Paducah.

But you cannot plan for water unless you
plan for land: for the cut-over mountains—
the eroded hills—the gullied fields that
pour their waters unchecked down to the river.

The CCC, working with the forest service and
agricultural experts, have started to put the
worn fields and hillsides back together; black
walnut and pine for the worn out fields, and
the gullied hillsides; black walnut and pine
for new forest preserves, roots for the cut-
over and burned-over hillsides; roots to hold
the water in the ground.

Soil conservation men have worked out crop
systems with the farmers of the Valley—
crops to conserve and enrich the topsoil.

Today a million acres of land in the
Tennessee Valley are being tilled scientifically.

But you cannot plan for water and land unless
you plan for people. Down in the Valley, the
Farm Security Administration has built a model
agricultural community. Living in homes they
themselves built, paying for them on long term
rates the homesteaders will have a chance to
share in the wealth of the Valley.

More important, the Farm Security Administration has lent thousands of dollars to farmers
in the Valley, farmers who were caught by years

of depression and in need of only a stake to be self sufficient.

But where there is water there is power.

Where there's water for flood control and water for navigation, there's water for power—

Power for the farmers of the Valley.

Power for the villages and cities and factories of the Valley.

West Virginia, North Carolina, Tennessee, Mississippi, Georgia and Alabama.

Power to give a new Tennessee Valley to a new generation.

Power enough to make the river work!

THE

MAKING

OF *ECCE*

HOMO

BEHOLD

THE MAN

I had been told by officials of the U.S. Department of Agriculture that they did not wish to continue producing motion pictures. So part of the spring of 1938 I spent running about Washington looking for a new home and production money.

During this time I received a telephone call from Bill Lewis, the head of radio production at Columbia Broadcasting System. He was a gracious, intelligent man, and he propositioned me in several ways, finally asking me if I'd like to be the head of a one-hour Sunday weekly radio magazine.

Although the money was tempting indeed compared with what I was making, I didn't wish to leave government service as long as Mr. Roosevelt endorsed my work. Finally, at the end of one meeting Lewis said that he'd like me to come over and try out any ideas I might have and recommended that I use the Columbia Workshop under Bill Robson as a place for my experiments.

Shortly after I was solicited by Bill Lewis, King Vidor came to New York on his way to England and said that he had an extra cabin ticket on the *Manhattan*, as Spencer Tracy had suddenly backed out of going to England to play the lead part in King's movie *The Citadel*. He also said he was having a little trouble with the shooting script of the movie and maybe we could talk about it on the way to England.

I called the White House and spoke with Tom Corcoran and asked if it was all right if I took a long weekend in England and that I was dog-tired from exhibiting and promoting *The River* up and down the land.

Tom said, "Wait a minute. I want to speak with the president about it." After a minute or so he came back and said: "The president said you deserve a vacation but be sure and come right back. He's going to give you the world with a red fence around it."

He didn't explain what *that* was, but it was the establishment of the U.S. Film Service he was talking about, which became a reality with the directive of August 13, 1938, establishing such a service and making me its head.

I had a great time with Vidor in London and exhibited *The River,* which by chance was on the *Manhattan.* Iris Berry, the head of the Museum of Modern Art Film Library, had cabled John Grierson and Robert Flaherty to meet me, which they did. It was after seeing *The River* that Flaherty told me he would like to come to America and work for the U.S. government, adding: "I left the U.S. because of Herbert Hoover and now I would like to leave the British Empire because I'm tired of their understatement."

The British visit is another story.

Having my portable typewriter with me, I spent several hours a day working on a comprehensive outline of the radio script of "Ecce Homo," which I planned to present to Bill Robson. In the radio program I wanted to try out both the theme and the style of my proposed movie. This was not a new idea for me, because I had written a lyrical version of *The River* for *McCall's* magazine long before I had finished editing the movie.

Bill Robson was a wonderful man to work with—intelligent, high-spirited, generous, and greatly admired by the staff people I met at CBS. We worked with Bernard Herrmann on sound effects and music ideas, including the themes I chose for the gut sequences of the radio show, which was the meeting of four unemployed men from four regions of the United States: north, east, south, and west.

The four men meet at a filling station in Kansas and to the accompaniment of music from their regions, they deliver soliloquies on conditions they are leaving. For New England, I chose the hymn that starts "There is a fountain full of blood." For the South, the negro chain gang song based on an old hymn that starts out, "Every little step gets you nearer and nearer." For the West, Virgil Thomson agreed to let me use his adaptation of the theme of *The Plow That Broke the Plains*: "I'm Leaving Old Texas Now." Finally, the protagonist, Worker Number 7790 (who was an unemployed actor named Van Heflin), spoke his soliloquy to the accompaniment of sound effects of the assembly line.

This was a bi-election year—1938—and the hate campaign against President Roosevelt's New Deal was gaining strength, so Bill Robson and I figured we'd best not circulate my script around CBS. We didn't even show the finished script to Bill Lewis until before luncheon on the Saturday of the broadcast; as it turned out, Bill had tickets for a doubleheader at Yankee Stadium between the Yankees and Cleveland. He had a choice either of going to the ball game or reading our radio play. He chose to go to the ball game, but after he heard the broadcast, he told us that had he read the script, he would have cancelled the show.

As far as the notices were concerned, they were excellent. Some very favorable fan letters were received from listeners responding to the request for comments made by the CBS announcer at the end of my broadcast.

As for criticism, CBS had a very direct one in the form of the cancellation by Ford Company of its advertising program with CBS.

I had nothing but help, encouragement, and merriment working with Bill Robson, and we planned several other shows, which we never got around to presenting to Bill Lewis because the experimental show that followed "Ecce Homo" was the Orson Welles production "Invasion from Mars."

RCA made some records for me, which I took to Washington and gave to Tom Corcoran, and I presume he played them for Mr. Roosevelt, as the president seemed to be aware of the contents of "Ecce Homo" when I saw him when I presented my finished movie *The Fight for Life* at the White House on New Year's Eve, 1939.

Somewhere along the line Alistair Cooke made arrangements with CBS to have "Ecce Homo" broadcast by the British Broadcasting Corporation. It was produced by Laurence Gilliam with Alistair Cooke advising.

The BBC changed the title to "Job to Be Done" without asking CBS's or my permission. They were so gracious about *The River* I never did complain to them. I think they did it because "Ecce Homo" is a part of the Catholic religious ceremony; presumably it is what Pontius Pilate said when Jesus was brought before him.

My reason for the title was I recall having read many years ago that Leonardo da Vinci considered his statue of a man which he entitled "Ecce Homo" to be his greatest piece of work. It was destroyed by a vanguard of troops of Francis I. They in turn were killed because of their vandalism.

Another change they made which irked me was that some BBC writer could not stand "Mama" not ever having a word to say but just scurrying around carrying out the orders of the old man of the filling station.

I have a studio recording of "Ecce Homo" given me by CBS and several sets of records made from that recording by RCA, and recently I have had a cassette tape made. As far as I know the production script of "Ecce Homo" never has been reproduced in the United States. The one herewith is copied from the September 1938 issue of *SEE World Film News*, London, England.

CBS paid me for only one performance of "Ecce Homo." I don't recall any of the details of the BBC arrangements with CBS, but I know that both Bill Lewis and Bill Robson were forthright in making our arrangements, and both were aware that I was rehearsing a theme and sound effects for my proposed U.S. government film.

We never did complete the motion picture, but it was not a total loss of work, as the industrial footage and the footage of the Columbia River gorges and of the construction of Grand Coulee Dam all were used by the Office of War Information during the Second World War.

The simple philosophy of "Ecce Homo" was that with the gigantic industrial equipment and the magnificent amount of arable land in our country, it was stupid to have eleven million to fifteen million unemployed men and women. The protagonist, Worker Number 7790, was *technologically* unemployed. He was able-bodied, a war veteran, uninterested in labor politics or social philosophy. It was through his working his way across the country from east to west that I was going to show the power of the machinery and the beauty of the land, accompanied by the music of the regions of America.

: : :

I will never forget one Sunday in July (July 13, 1938) because of the way the president greeted me when I walked into his office. Tom Corcoran had called me and told me the president wanted to talk with me about a movie program. The directive establishing the U.S. Film Service in the National Emergency Council had not yet been written, but the *New York Times* on June 18 had printed a correct story that this was to take place.

Tom asked me to stop by his quarters on the way to the White House Sunday morning so that he could have a look at what I wanted to show the president. He read the outline for the movie *Ecce Homo* and, being a musician, he turned to me and said, "I guess you'll have to find a Beethoven to write the score for *that* movie." He said he couldn't go with me but gave me instructions when to walk into the president's office and told me that if the press asked me what I was doing on my way in to see the president, I was to show them the little award plaque from the Independent Theater Owners of America who had voted *The River* the most popular and successful box-office-draw short motion picture of the year.

When I was ushered into the office, the president greeted me with a broader than usual smile and said, "Well, Pare, I see in this morning's paper that you have been nominated for a Pulitzer Prize in poetry."

I knew of no such news story. I had worked late typing out the outline and I hadn't seen the morning paper, much less the *Herald Tribune Book Review Section*. The president, seeing my astonishment, enlightened me in a fatherly tone by saying Lewis Gannett had reviewed the book of *The River* and had nominated it for the prize.

When I showed the president the award plaque, he made some kind of Harvard joke about the statue itself, because it was of a nude man with some kind of shield for his midsection which appeared to be underwear. Getting down to business, the president then ebulliently said he wanted me to make about thirty little three- to five-minute movies about pending public works programs. When he finished outlining this program, I told him, to his obvious annoyance, that I did not want to do this. I did, I said, on the other hand, want to make a big two-hour feature film.

Before explaining the theme of my proposed movie, I told him that we had managed to get thirty minutes' exposure on the commercial screen with both *The Plow That Broke the Plains* and *The River*. If we cut our work down to three minutes or five minutes per picture, we would be flashed on the screen against at least four hours of double-feature Hollywood movies and thus would in no way leave an impact on audiences. On the other hand, if we put all the basic problems of public works into one big powerful message, audiences would understand the philosophy underlying the government policy.

I then presented the president with the few pages of general outline, except for the last page, which I kept in my pocket. He read it carefully and then asked me, "How are you going to end it?"

I said, rather impudently, "Sir, how are *you* going to end it?" Then I showed him the last page, which was simply an endorsement of regional development of the United States based on the Tennessee Valley Authority idea. He was most enthusiastic and ended as he always did, I imagine, with all visitors: "Come back and see me again."

Although the U.S. Film Service was still a month away from being made a part of the National Emergency Council, the head of which was to be a former managing editor of the Scripps Howard tabloid in Washington, Lowell Mellett, the president had approved my project and I was able to keep my business manager, Arch Mercey, my secretary, and some of the clerical people in charge of distribution of *The Plow* and *The River* who were to be moved out of the Agricultural Department and over to my new organization. In that month I was allowed to scurry about making arrangements to visit Grand Coulee Dam and to meet the man President Roosevelt wanted to put in charge of the Columbia River development, namely, J. D. Ross. I had my request for permissions to work in industrial plants sent out to key outfits in the industrial Middle West and had regional information men help me get those permissions in person.

ECCE	Written and directed by Pare Lorentz
HOMO	Produced by the Columbia Workshop under the direction of William N. Robson
BEHOLD	
THE MAN	Music by Bernard Herrmann
	Narrator: Thomas Chalmers

Narrator: This is industrial America.

(A chugging discordant, syncopated sound effect throughout this litany)

Statistician: Boston: boots and shoes, fish and wool.

Narrator: Streamers and dies, silk and paper, sewing machines and motorcycles.

Narrator: Waterbury—Bridgeport.

Statistician: Airplanes and ammunition, brass fittings and cotton shirts, submarines and watches.

Narrator: Paterson—Jersey City.

Statistician: Paint and varnish, Vaseline and patent medicine, electric wire and asphalt, leather goods and silk.

Narrator: Philadelphia—Camden.

Statistician: Radios and locomotives, street cars and carpets, chemicals and furniture, hosiery and turbines, children's clothes and boilers.

Narrator: Pittsburgh—Wheeling.

Statistician: Tin plate and fire brick, air brakes and plumbing fixtures, tube steel and freight cars, anthracite and mine machinery, aluminum and plate glass, drawing instruments and tacks.

Narrator: Buffalo—Syracuse.

Statistician: Tin cans and soda ash, mince meat and typewriters, washing machines and light bulbs.

Narrator: Cleveland—Youngstown.

Statistician: Nuts and bolts and printing presses, diesel engines and multigraph machines, electric batteries and steel forgings.

Narrator: Akron—Toledo.

Statistician: Airplane motors and rubber tires, beer bottles and spark plugs, steel hooks and microphones, spray guns and paper bags.

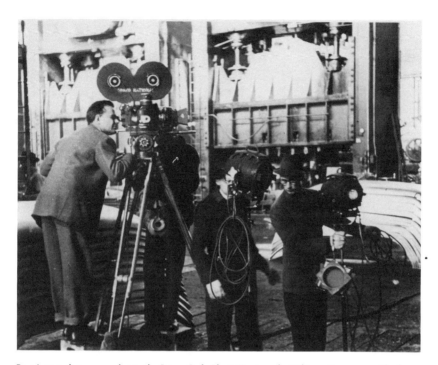

Pare Lorentz lining up a shot in the Briggs Body Plant, Hamtramck, Michigan. Cameraman Floyd Crosby is on the far right, handling lights.

Narrator: This is industrial America!
    Detroit—Pontiac.

Statistician: Automobiles and trailers, trucks and buses, taxicabs and coaches, draft forgings and steel bushings, carburetors and paint, coal stokers and tear gas bombs.

Narrator: Chicago—Gary.

Statistician: Bacon and beef, telephones and furniture and pipe organs, doors and sashes, marine motors and cotton gloves, transmission chains and saws.

Narrator: Indianapolis—South Bend.

Statistician: Threshing machines and whiskey, tractors and ball bearings, fruit jars and lawnmowers, outboard motors and ornamental fences.

Narrator: Kansas City—St. Louis.

Plymouth assembly line workers' automobiles parked in a street in Hamtramck while they are at work, January 1938. From Ecce Homo.

Statistician: Grain elevators and pipelines, Pullman cars and beer, plows and rugs and breakfast foods.

Narrator: Minneapolis—St. Paul.

Statistician: Silos and skis, macaroni and mattresses, cattle scales.

Narrator: This is industrial America, the power and glory of the richest country in the world. A factory of seven million men and women.

Foreman: Worker Number 7785
          Worker Number 7786
          Worker Number 7787
          Worker Number 7788
          Worker Number 7789
          Worker Number 7790
(Sound of nut-runners; industrial music continuing underneath)

Girl worker, Eaton Axle Plant, Cleveland, Ohio, January 1939. From Ecce Homo.

Statistician: Ladies and gentlemen, this is the straight line. In two
minutes, before your very eyes, you will see thirty thousand
different pieces of material assembled into one machine.

Two weeks ago these parts were still in the mines of
Pennsylvania and West Virginia, the oil fields of Texas and
Oklahoma and the copper shafts of Montana, the iron mountains
of Minnesota.

They have come from the strip mills of Ohio, from the textile
mills of the South, tested and checked, processed and perfected
in straight lines as intricate as this.

Along these two steel tracks half a mile long, you will see
steel, iron, glass, tin, lead, zinc, aluminum, chromium and
nickel.

You will see rubber, mica, glass, cotton, mohair, all set into
place, magically assembled into one tested, perfect piece of
machinery, the American automobile. Two days ago these parts
were moving through a hundred factories, on a hundred straight

Worker inside body jig, Plymouth assembly line, Hamtramck, January 1939. From Ecce Homo.

lines; they received the skill of thousands of men and women, in order that they might reach this assembly plant in a state of perfection.

You will see a new car drive off the line every half a minute. Here, through the vigilance and skill of workers, inspectors, managers and scientists, men and machines create a perfect instrument. Here is a saga of human ingenuity, planning and coordination, the glory of industrial America.

Statistician: Here is the straight line!

Foreman: Number 7735.

Statistician: Engine block and valve seat.

Foreman: Number 7738.

Statistician: Crankshaft and connecting rod.

Foreman: Number 7740.

Statistician: Fenders and hood.

Foreman: Number 7743.

Statistician: Rear springs.

Foreman: Number 7745.

Statistician: Rear axle and differential.

Foreman: Number 7748.

Statistician: Shock absorbers and gas tank.

Foreman: Number 7750.

Statistician: Front axle and springs.

Foreman: Number 7754.

Statistician: Drive shaft and transmission.

Foreman: Number 7757.

Statistician: Engine block and insulation.

Foreman: Number 7760.

Statistician: Crankshaft and valve seat.

Foreman: Number 7764.

Statistician: Piston and connecting rod.

Foreman: Number 7766.

Statistician: Spray paint and drying oven.

Foreman: Number 7780.

Statistician: Brake tubing.

Foreman: Number 7783.

Statistician: Wheels and tires.

Foreman: Number 7785.

Statistician: Steering gear and radiator.

Foreman: Number 7788.

Statistician: Doors and braces.

Sign in the Briggs Manufacturing Company body plant, January 1939. From Ecce Homo.

Foreman: 7790.

Statistician: Tires and top welding.
   (Music stops temporarily)

Sales Manager: Time study department?
   Watson in Sales speaking. We're forty-five hundred units off this
   week. Right.

Time Study Man: Production?
   Jenkins in Time Studies. We're forty-five hundred units off. I'm
   sending the breakdown over.

Production Manager: Hello, Casey?
   Production. We're cutting down to three days a week.

Chorus: LAYOFF-LAYOFF-LAYOFF-LAYOFF-LAYOFF-LAYOFF-
   LAYOFF-LAYOFF-LAYOFF-LAYOFF.
   (Soft volume builds to final shouts)

WPA Clerk: Number 7790: application for release, name?
   (Checking machine punctuates questions and answers)

7790: Jack Latham.

WPA Clerk: Age.

7790: 43.

WPA Clerk: Height.

7790: Six foot one.

WPA Clerk: Weight.

7790: 185 pounds.

WPA Clerk: Place of birth.

7790: Louisa, Kentucky.

WPA Clerk: Father.

7790: Dead.

WPA Clerk: Mother.

7790: Dead.

WPA Clerk: Married or single.

7790: Single.

WPA Clerk: Served in U.S. Army, Navy or Marine Corps.

7790: Sergeant—U.S. Army Infantry, 386th regiment, 77th division.

WPA Clerk: Present employment.

7790: None.

WPA Clerk: Real estate.

7790: None.

WPA Clerk: Ever insured.

7790: Yes.

WPA Clerk: Any insurance now.

7790: None.

WPA Clerk: Property other than household goods.

7790: Automobile.

WPA Clerk: Any income from blind or old age pension, lodges, labor unions, U.S. Government or other source.

7790: None.

WPA Clerk: Cash securities, stocks and bonds, mortgages, certificates.

7790: Cash—$35
No other securities, etc.

> 7790—First paper passed.
> 7790—First application for relief passed (Loud)
> 7790-7790-7790-7790-7790-7790-7790 (fades out)

Narrator: 7790 is headed west.
7790, west on highway 40.
(We hear for the first time 7790 soliloquizing)

Narrator: West of Gary, west of Chicago Heights and Aurora.

7790: 7790 is headed west in a '36 sedan with thirty-five bucks in his pocket. (Music fades in—medley of popular songs 1917–1927—ends with Black Bottom.)
Name—Age—Occupation. I remember when we went down to the courthouse. You could see the pines stretching clear across to Virginia then. You could kick a pheasant out of a laurel bush. You could go hook a bass at the head of the ripples and hoe a corn patch all in one day. I remember when we went down to the courthouse. They had the old boys march with us. And I remember how Judge Adams got red in the face and waved his arms.
Going to France to save the women and children.
They kept picking up Ben Davis and putting him on the steps. Boy, was he drunk!
I remember the kids didn't go to school. They stood on the freight cars and waved their little flags when the trains pulled out. Yeah, it was hot in Chillicothe.

Narrator: 7790 riding with a million men on wheels.

Stat: The cottonpickers riding on route 90; out of New Orleans to Houston, through to San Antone, north to Oklahoma and Arizona and the new cotton fields.

7790: When we came home we used to sit on the courthouse steps and watch for the new cars going through town.

They said there was a war, but they cut down the trees while we were away and set up electric light poles on Main Street.

They said times were different.

The chemical plant killed the bass clear down past Black's Falls and you walked ten miles to find a clear stream.

They put up a French 75 on the courthouse square.

We used to sit all day Sunday talking and looking at the new cars.

Narrator: 7790 riding on the highway of the unemployed.

Stat: The fruit tramps riding on the desert road, over from Jacksonville, across the continent, clear to California. Up route 99 for lemons and oranges, prunes and peaches. Up past Fresno and Washington and Oregon for apples.

7790: The man said he'd give us all a hundred dollars and our railroad fare. Said they needed strong boys in the north. They gave us ten dollars a day in Akron. We bought silk shirts and got drunk every night and slept at the machines and the foreman used to throw wrenches at us.

It was crazy then. You could spend all night at the amusement park and buy silk shirts.

In the body plant you could get twenty dollars if you worked hard.

We were twenty-seven then.

I remember that tough inspector in Detroit. He caught me sitting down and he chased me clear out of the plant and they had my check waiting at the cage as I went by.

Narrator: 7790 riding west on route 80, picking lettuce, peas, onions and spinach.

Up 87 to Denver and Sheraton.

Along the side of the Rockies to Billings and Great Falls to the sugar beet fields.

(Music fade in.)

7790: I remember in '27 when the production department said we couldn't weld zinc. We got gas tanks going in six weeks and he gave us a bonus.

They put on short time and the married men only got four days a week.

Then they put that twenty-ton press in plant #10 and got kids to stamp out tops and fenders.

Narrator: 7790 heading west.

Stat: West across the Mississippi.

The wheat men heading west on route 10 to Minneapolis.

West across the northern tabletop to Fargo and Grand Falls, Valley City and Bismarck.

Over the divide to Missoula and Spokane.

7790: Name—Age—Occupation.

(Coda music fades in.)

They'll sit around the union halls and the married men get the first relief cards.

They'll go to meetings and the old men will get the first short time.

They'll talk politics and play cards and wait for the food cards.

But there's a country in the west I've never seen.

They say the youngsters get all the jobs except the youngsters never carried duckboards in France with mud up to their knees.

They say the bums go west, but they're building dams in the desert. They're cutting down mountains!

Narrator: 7790 riding with a million men on wheels.

Statistician: Coffee and hamburgers 10 cents.

We fix flats.

Chicken dinners and tourist cabins; second-hand tires; free water; hot dogs and pop.

Today's special—pork and beans 15 cents.

Do drop in! Coffee free to truck drivers.

Hollywood cabins 50 cents a night.

Tourist farm—free lights and water.

Welcome to the city. Rotary luncheon—12:00 on Tuesday.

Second-hand tires! Free water and air! We fix flats!

Lodging house off Michigan Avenue, Detroit, Michigan, February 1939. From Ecce Homo.

(Music ends in loud dissonant chord.)

(7790 and three other unemployed men meet at a Kansas City roadside filling station; one from New England, one from Alabama and one from the Texas Panhandle. Under each soliloquy there is music of the region. Under New England a hymn "How Firm a Foundation." Under Alabama a chain gang work song, the hymn "Every Little Step Gets You Nearer." Under the Texan, Virgil Thomson's "I'm Leaving Old Texas Now" from *The Plow That Broke the Plains*.)

Filling Station Operator: Hi there fella. What'll it be?

7790: Well, fill her up.

Filling Station Operator: Yes sir. Ya come from the East?

7790: Yep.

Filling Station Operator: Ya going far?

7790: Well, pretty far.

Filling Station Operator: Well, y'll have lots of company. I was telling a fella the other day: So many people on the highway, I said, wonders to me that there's anybody at home at all!

Well, that'll be a dollar ten with tax. What else can I do for you?

7790: Give me a box of crackers, a coke and some cheese.

Filling Station Operator: Store cheese or rat cheese?

7790: Store cheese.

Filling Station Operator: Mama, bring out a box of those crackers and some store cheese.

Hey come on over here and sit in the shade, brother. We've got the best shade in Kansas I always say.

7790: Thanks, I believe I will.
(Sound of car arriving)

Filling Station Operator: Ah whooooooooee.
Looks like I've got another customer.
Well, hi there. Fill her up?

Texan: No sir, Three gallons would be about right.

Filling Station Operator: Yes, sir.

Texan: I say, you got a small crowbar around here I can borrow?

Filling Station Operator: Hey Mama, where's that little crowbar I had last week?

7790: Look on the floor in the back seat of my sedan and you'll find one.

Texan: Why thanks.

Filling Station Operator: Yeah, that'll be forty-six cents with tax. Hmmmmm, having trouble with your tires?

Texan: Yep, bent a rim running on a flat. Mind if I fix it here?

Filling Station Operator: Sure, sure, go right ahead. Yeah, I'll sit over here in the shade and watch ya. Well—ho-ho-ho—yes, sir, it's the best shade in Kansas.

7790: Feels good to me after that hot road.

Filling Station Operator: Yeah, You said you're from the East, huh?

7790: Yep.

Filling Station Operator: Well, how is it back there?

7790: Well, it's sorta quiet.

Filling Station Operator: I've never been East, but I was telling Mama the other day: a man sittin' right here on this porch can just meet people from all over.

Now take the other day. I was sittin' here and I looked down the road, and, well, it was hot, just as hot as it is today.

And I see a woman carrying a violin and a man carrying a baby coming down the road. Well sir, that doggone baby weren't more than about a year old. They come a-dragging in—young people they was—and I asked them wheres they were from and ya know where? California.

Well, seeings how they come so far I asked them in to set awhile. Well, it seems this fella played in a band but it went broke. "How far are you going?" I said. East he said. "How far East?" I said. Well, the girl said she's got an aunt in Brooklyn, clear in New York.

They hadn't seen her in ten years but they figured she was around somewhere and she'd put 'em up.

Well, Mama gave 'em one of our fifty-cent cabins and fed em up and we got them a ride with a fella going into Chicago.

But I told Mama, I says, I'd sure like to see that aunt's face when they walked in with that baby.

Texan: Thanks for the use of the crowbar, partner.

7790: That's all right. You got it fixed already?

Texan: Yeah, I think I'll sit down in the shade and just cool off.

Filling Station Operator: Sit down, sit down. Like I told this fella, best shade in Kansas.

Texan: Yeah, feels good to me.
(Sound of car arriving)

Filling Station Operator: My goodness! Look at that old boy! Mama, bring out that watercan. Got a fella on fire out here.

Alabaman: I thought it got hot in Alabama, but this Kansas, now it's *really* hot.

Filling Station Operator: Brother, this is midwinter to what it was in '36. Now that's when it was hot.

I was sitting right here on this porch when old man Jones, he's got two sections of land west over there, he comes running in to call the Abilene fire department. His wheat field just naturally blew up and caught fire somehow.

It's the gospel truth. Spontaneous combustion or something they said—Just give it to the man, Mama.

Alabaman: Thank you Ma'am.

Filling Station Operator: Hey, you'd better cool it off before you put that in or you'll have spontaneous combustion. (Sound of car arriving)

Well—hi there. Yes, sir, what'll it be?

New Englander: Why, I'd thank you for some drinking water if you've got any around and a can of tobacco.

Filling Station Operator: Well, just go right inside, brother and Mama will take care of you.

7790: I'd like some of that water myself.

Filling Station Operator: There's a bucket and a dipper on the porch. Just help yourself. Best water in Kansas I always say.

7790: Thanks.

Alabaman: A Trailer's no use to a man unless he's got a family. You oughta travel alone if you want to get somewhere. You heading east?

New Englander: I'm going West. I'm aiming for Iowa.

Alabaman: I'm heading East and I thought maybe I could find some company. My old grandmother always said poor people ought to travel together. I'm heading East.

(Hymn music fades in under soliloquy)

New Englander: I'm from the East and I'll tell you about it.

My partner and I, we set machinery in the biggest textile mill on the Bay.

There's no two better mill mechanics in New England we used
to say.

When they shut the mills down in '31, we watched them setting
there with their broken windows, just like blind, gray old men.
And the fog drifting in from the Vineyard.

Yeah, we sat there and watched them. Then we took summer
people for boat rides and we fished for bait and waited.

We helped them tear down the machinery.

The mills is moving south, they said, but we're New England men.

So we bought a trailer. We went over to the lakes.

They'll need new men in the factories we said.

It's cold in Michigan.

My partner had a dog. But we gave him to a fella and got a cat.
The cat could find its own food.

Well, they didn't need mechanics they said. Then we sold the
trailer. My partner took his share and went home. Went on relief I
figured.

But I'm heading South where the mills is. If they're cotton mills
they'll need machinists, I told him.

(Hymn music out. Chain gang song fades in.)

Alabaman: Yep, there's work in the south. Brother, there's work in
the south.

There's work for eight million people planting cotton, chopping
cotton, picking cotton, following the sun in the hot fields.

There's work in the new cotton mills, work enough at eight
dollars a week. The lint choking ya and the kids and the store
man leaving ya behind every Saturday.

My granddaddy came over from Carolina before my daddy was
born. Cleared himself a place in the pines. His people raised
cotton before then. In '17 we had 150 acres in the clear.

Then cotton went from fifty cents to six cents in a week. The
bank was busted.

We held on but we had to go shares in '30.

Ain't never been ahead since.

Sometimes it seems like the very fields are tired.

Now they're talking about chopping cotton with machines.

Well, when my womenfolk went to the mills I said—I'm going
North.

Surplus commodities line, Cleveland, Ohio, January 1939. From Ecce Homo.

Why, I read that a fella up there died and left nine billion dollars.

I says I'm going North where the mills pay you enough for radios and movies. I said I'm going up where the money is!

(Chain gang music fades out. Bernard Herrmann's industrial score in.)

7790: They say they're jumping off bridges in Akron.

They say they're mumbling in the breadlines.

But the machines and the men are there. I remember when they told us you've got to cut up forty ships. And I remember the Swede rigged up jigsaws and we cut 'em down two a week.

I'm heading West where they're moving mountains.

(*The Plow That Broke the Plains* music sneaks in.)

Texan: They took me West when I was six years old. My father moved me from Missouri. They said my lungs was bad, that the river was bad for my lungs.

You could see the tan grass waving for fifty miles out there then.

At night I used to cry when the Rock Island whistled across the plains and the coyotes answered.

I used to cry and once I tried to run away.

Then they gave me a pony and a heifer of my own. I never wanted to go back to Missouri.

When I was twenty-one my father gave me a section of land. My brother and I ran three sections in '17.

Then we went to war and they plowed up the land. My father was patriotic, said they'd plowed it all while we were away. They brought the tractors and combines.

Fellas used to come clear from Chicago, plant a crop, go away. Suitcase farmers we called them.

They used to plow a thousand acres a week, before the dust came.

We stuck it six years. We sat six years and watched the dust.

We watched the dust drift over the windows. It took all Fall to push the dust off the fields so you could raise another crop of dust the next Spring.

So, we hit the highway in '36.

I'll tell you about the West.

There's work cutting grapes at ten cents a tray.

Money for gas enough to get you to the next camp.

There's work picking cotton at ten cents an hour, living in a migratory camp, eating beans and meat the butcher throws away.

And there's the nights in camp with the children crying and the woman staring at you so a man can't stand it.

I said I'd drown mine before I'd raise kids that way.

So I'm heading for Iowa.

My wife's following the crop with my brother.

But I'm leaving the kids with kin in Iowa so they'll know what a home's like. Maybe I'll go back.

(Industrial music)

7790: They had to let the dynamiters down the side of the canyon on ropes at Boulder Dam.

They blew up a mountain and made a lake and a desert and built the highest dam in the world.

New Englander: But you can't eat dams.

They're changing the course of one of the biggest rivers in the country at Grand Coulee.

"They had to let the dynamiters down the side of the canyon on ropes at Boulder Dam."
From Ecce Homo.

Pare Lorentz (left) talking with the foreman of the jackhammer crew, Grand Coulee Dam, August 1938.

Alabaman: Yeah, but they can't figure out how to feed eleven million of us.

7790: They hit quicksand up there so they stuck brine pipes in there and froze her, and then dug it out.

(The "Battle Hymn of the Republic" orchestral music begins from low volume and deliberate tempo and swells to marching/fighting instead of triumphant tempo and volume as the final words of hope are spoken by 7790 ending with the chorus singing the first stanza of "The Battle Hymn of the Republic")

Texan: The big boys have the machines. There's nothing but relief for the little man.

7790: There's men and machines and there's room. There'll be water enough for thousands of farms up there.

New Englander: Yep, but the big boys have the money.

7790: There's room enough for thirty million people.

Why, man, they're building the biggest piece of machinery in the world.

Alabaman: But what'll they do when they finish?

(Music now swells in volume)

They can build plenty more!
They can make the desert green!
Maybe they'll build a green city.
Maybe they'll start East and build her all over again.
Maybe there'll be farms for the little man!
They can move mountains and they can shove rivers around!
There's men and machines and there's sun and land and room for a man to turn around in.
And there's a man-sized job to be done!

(Chorus and orchestra.)

Mine eyes have seen the glory of the coming of the Lord;
He is trampling out the vintage where the grapes of wrath are stored;
He hath loosed the fateful lightning of his terrible swift sword;
His truth is marching on.
Glory! Glory! Hallelujah!
Glory! Glory! Hallelujah!
Glory! Glory! Hallelujah!
His truth is marching on.

I was graduated from the U.S. Army Air Force Officers Training School, Miami Beach, Florida, January 9, 1943, and was immediately stationed at the headquarters of the Air Transport Command at the annex building, National Airport in Washington, D.C. I had been invited to the Second World War by General C. R. Smith, deputy commanding officer of the Air Transport Command, and by his superior, General Harold L. George, commanding general. My mission, as set forth in General George's first order to me, was "to work with operations officers in obtaining complete aerial and ground briefing pictures of interior and overseas air installations and routes operated or used by the Air Transport Command, and to record in complete pictorial detail the terrain, personnel, operations, and work performed by the Air Transport Command in any theatre or area designated by the Chief of Staff." (That we did.)

I had not been on duty very many days when I was peremptorily ordered to report to Air Corps Intelligence at headquarters in the Pentagon. I was greeted at intelligence by a well-knit, short, stern-faced intelligence officer, who immediately got down to business. He pulled a file out of his desk drawer, meantime asking me, "Do you know John Steinbeck?"

I said yes, I did, I knew him pretty well, and I asked what was the problem with John.

Without any explanation, he opened up the file which began with a letter from President Franklin D. Roosevelt to Secretary of War Henry L. Stimson. It was a breezy, short, familiar note and as I recall began with "Dear Hank."

I did not copy anything, and it has been forty-nine years since I saw the material, but I remember that the letter said that the president wished John Steinbeck to be given a major's commission in the U.S. Army Air Corps, as he was about to write a book about the strict and comprehensive training bomber crews were given before they went into combat, with the main purpose of informing the parents of such crews and the general public as to the pains that were being taken to save as many lives of our airmen as possible. He also said he'd like this done right away.

The next letter was one from Secretary Stimson to General Arnold, and it was very polite and very formal and merely without comment forwarded the president's request. The next letter was from General Arnold to whoever was in charge of personnel, and it was an informal yet positive order for the subordinate to hurry up and commission Steinbeck as a major in the U.S. Army Air Corps.

The fourth letter the officer turned over he didn't let me read but just see in time to notice that it was from the U.S. Navy to either General Arnold or to the chief intelligence officer of the Air Corps. I was not allowed to read it, but in general it was obvious the navy had said that Steinbeck either was a Communist or was a friend of Communists and should not be allowed to serve in the Air Corps.

I was startled and then outraged. I expressed my outrage to the officer by saying that I couldn't understand why the U.S. Navy thought it could overrule the commander in chief of all the U.S. forces, namely the president of the United States.

I noticed one letter under the navy letter signed Nunnally Johnson. I was asked if I knew him. I said I knew him quite well. Without a smile, the officer let me read the letter. It was short and to the point. It said, "You asked me if John Steinbeck drinks. Yes, he does, but not as much as General Grant." The intelligence officer didn't smile. I told him that certainly sounded like Nunnally and that he had worked very hard to retain all the virtues of Steinbeck's novel when he had done the movie script of *The Grapes of Wrath* and had succeeded very well indeed.

I was questioned for five or ten minutes about my association with John and whether I knew if he was or was not a Communist, which I didn't know one way or the other, as we had never discussed such a matter. I continued to politely abuse the Army Air Corps for not following the command of our commanding officer and for letting the navy meddle in *our* affairs.

The first time I was able to get a weekend leave to spend with my wife in our apartment in New York City, I located John and asked him to meet me. We took one of our usual long talking/walking trips through Central Park. He may have known about being turned down, but I'm not sure he knew it was the navy that was responsible. He looked sad and tired after he heard my report and said the only thing he could figure out was that there was only one Communist vote in their precinct in Los Gatos the last general election, and that he always figured his wife, Carol, had registered as a Communist just in order to enrage the association of farmers who publicly had declared against John's *The Grapes of Wrath* even before it was published.

I begged my old friend to call some of the ranking officials on the White House staff and tell them of the navy action, and I said that if I knew the president, he would surely take action and get John his commission. I didn't know whether John had by then married Gwyn or at least had been divorced by Carol, but it was clear that he didn't want to have to reveal any personal problems if it came up to an open fight with navy intelligence.

It was the last time we had a long walk-and-talk time together, although I did encounter him after the war going in and out of restaurants and taverns, where we spoke politely to each other. The last time, he was going into the 21 Club as I was coming out, and he stopped and we blocked the threshold for a few minutes while we passed the time of day. Finally he said, "Why don't you come over to the Bedford and I'll make us some coffee?" He made the strongest and best coffee I ever have tasted. It was "Cousin Jack" mining camp coffee made with egg shells; his judgment of the amount of water, the amount of coffee, the amount of egg shells, and the time of boiling was splendid. His invitation meant that he was writing and was holed up as he always did at the Bedford when he was working.

I don't know who originally recommended this little residential hotel to John and me—whether it was Otis Wiese, whose offices were at 230 Park Avenue, or whether it was one of John's wonderful agents at McIntosh and Otis: Elizabeth Otis, his literary agent, or Annie Laurie Williams, his theatrical agent in the firm. The Bedford is a small hotel on Fortieth Street, very near Grand Central Terminal. It was quiet and the suites had an efficient kitchen/pantry with high ceilings, a refrigerator, and plenty of utensils for cooking. It was as quiet as possible, given the location, and many writers and editors used it as a convenient hideaway for correcting or completing work. As I was living in the country in those days, and my editor was around the corner, I got to using the Bedford before I went into military service.

Recently I read John's credits and discovered he had written a book (which the president wanted him to do) called *Bombs Away!*

Our acquaintance started at his home in Los Gatos.

In the excellent presentation of John's journals, *Working Days*, kept while John was writing *The Grapes of Wrath*, Robert De Mott states that I met Carol Steinbeck in New York, where she was attending to business affairs connected with the disastrous opening of the play *Tortilla Flat*. I have no recollection of the place, but I do remember meeting Carol and the gentle but tough-minded lady agents, Misses Otis and Williams.

Carol was a big, loud, lanky, cheerful female who reminded me of many competent and similarly loud girls I knew from the hills and mountains of West Virginia, so we had a comfortable meeting. I evidently arranged for her a showing of *The Plow That Broke the Plains* and (possibly) *The River* for Steinbeck in Hollywood. On January 13, 1938, John wired Carol in New York, "Approve Lorentz affair greatly," according to De Mott.

After President Roosevelt saw *The River* at Hyde Park in September 1937, I had re-recorded *The River* at the Sam Goldwyn studios; opened *The River* to the press and the public for the first time in New Orleans in October 1937; had members of our information department preview *The River* at Memphis and Saint Louis; and, with my host and part-time cameraman, Professor Robert Kissack, had previewed the film to a standing-room-only audience at the Northrup Auditorium at the University of Minnesota. Finally, I had met with Mr. Barney Balaban of Balaban and Katz theatre chain in Chicago and had persuaded him to have a top-hat preview, with the result that he wired his endorsement of the film to Paramount Pictures headquarters in New York City.

I was booked to go to Hollywood to attempt to persuade United Artists to take the movie for commercial release when I met Carol. She made arrangements to get me to Los Gatos to meet John for the purpose of discussing with him a joint Steinbeck-Lorentz movie version of John's book *In Dubious Battle*. I was feeling out the possibility of making a commercial movie not because of the success of *The River*, but for any number of petty U.S. government reasons.

In 1936 the Resettlement Administration was made an integral part of the Department of Agriculture, and Dr. Will Alexander replaced Rex Tugwell as head of my organization; John Fischer replaced my original superior and supporter, John Franklin Carter; and once the Resettlement Administration had had its name changed to the Farm Security Administration, the purpose and broad policies of the agency had seemed to shrivel up inside the old walls of the Agriculture Department, where the outfit had been merged. John Fischer himself had called me to say that in the future the Department of Agriculture did not intend to produce movies, which was a polite way of getting rid of me.

The president had told Tom Corcoran in my presence to look after me, so I was not totally abandoned, but we were looking for a new home and new orders and I knew that when government money ran out on June 30 (the end of the government fiscal years in those days), I might be casting about for a worthwhile project as well as a livelihood.

I did not intend to leave government service if the president could find a place and money for me, but I didn't want to get thrown out of employment without having an ace in the hole. Furthermore, I was impressed and moved by *In Dubious Battle*. Not only was it full of vivid characterizations as well as flashes of pawky humor, but it also seemed to me then a complete tragedy in which the land holders, the land users, and the land workers all lost, and while I have not reread the book in many years, nor have I reread *The Grapes of Wrath* recently, I feel that perhaps *In Dubious Battle* is the best book John ever wrote.

I do not remember how I got to his home in Los Gatos, but I do remember it was during a tropical rainstorm that persisted throughout the first visit. When I was ushered into the one main room, John was working with an antique and dilapidated piece of machinery with which he was rolling his own cigarettes, and not very successfully, as he couldn't get them to stay rolled, even with a lot of twisting and licking the paper, and he was making a great show of insouciance every time his product disintegrated. He looked at me sideways with the wary expression of a suspicious but friendly sheep dog. He had a visitor, he explained, a young writer who lived, I think, either in a hollow tree or in an abandoned bear cave in Alaska or parts equally remote. John also had a handsome Gordon setter who was soggy and sad, but very obviously a good hunting dog. Anyway, after some polite small talk, John suddenly said, "Let's get the hell out of here and go to San Francisco."

I never had been to the great city of San Francisco, but as for that trip I could hardly say that I visited the city. It rained continuously all through the drive up, and we were deluged with spray as well as rain until we reached our destination, a tavern called John's Rendezvous. It was half underground, with a wine cellar, and built into a hillside, the cellar having an extra bar and a few tables for diners.

John had presciently called his friend Joseph Henry Jackson, of the *San Francisco Chronicle* (then the best newspaper in the state). Joe arrived with his wife, Charlotte, who, as the evening whizzed by started complaining about getting home because of the children and because the last trolley was going to leave for Berkeley, and they would have to take a taxi home, and so forth and so forth. Joe was one of the first important critics to inform East Coast editors about John's work, and the Jacksons and the Steinbecks were a great foursome who had traveled together to Mexico for several vacations. Joe and Charlotte and all those "children" (*they* turned out to be one delightful young lady named Marion) and we became good friends, and after Joe's untimely death we saw Charlotte and Marion both in their bright and comfortable home in Berkeley and in our apartment and in our home in the country in the East. We enjoyed many happy times.

All I can remember of the evening was that there was a strolling quartet of middle-aged men who claimed to have served in the British forces—in Mesopotamia in His Majesty's Royal Camel Corps. They sang Kipling's Barracks Room Ballads very well, and I discovered that Mr. Jackson was the head of the High-jinks Committee of the Bohemian Club, had a very good clear tenor voice, and knew just as many Methodist hymns as I did. The result was that Jackson missed the last trolley, and John drove us back to his home in the same storm, with the same spray, but more or less oblivious to the weather.

John Steinbeck had become a successful writer by the time I first met him. He had not only written five novels, but also had adapted one of them, *Of Mice and Men*, into a play which was playing on Broadway at the time and which his agents had sold to Metro-Goldwyn-Mayer. He may not have been famous, but he certainly was an established writer. In all my correspondence from John, he seldom wrote down a year, and sometimes he didn't even put in a month, so I have no record of our next meeting, which was in Hollywood.

I put him up where I was staying at the Beverly Wilshire Hotel. It was just possible he came to the preview of *The River*, which was a very elegant occasion, but I don't remember because we never talked about it. I do know that I had made arrangements for the opening of *The River* in New York City and that the opening took place at the Criterion Theatre on February 4, 1938, and I remember I missed that opening on purpose, as I was satisfied with the notices we had from up and down the Mississippi River and particularly from the Balaban and Katz organization in Chicago. I think they are greatly responsible for persuading Paramount Pictures to distribute my movie, and I think I signed a contract with Paramount in March or April after the splendid notices following the opened in New York City. Anyway, I know that I was with King and Betty Vidor in Ensenada, Baja California, at the time *The River* opening in New York City.

IN

DUBIOUS

BATTLE

It was during this interval that John was my guest in Hollywood while we attempted to make a deal for the production of *In Dubious Battle*. The first thing we did, I know, was to visit MGM, which had bought the dramatic rights to *Of Mice and Men*. Although Mervyn LeRoy was a Warner Brothers man, he had been hired by MGM to produce John's play. John was not unfamiliar with Los Angeles and Hollywood, but I don't think he had ever been to a movie studio before. I knew LeRoy casually and had greatly admired his movie *They Won't Forget*, which was about the Leo Frank case and was adapted from a novel by Ward Greene called *Death in the Deep South*. Many critics dwelt upon the brief, bouncy, and first appearance of Lana Turner. In my review of the movie (page 147 of *Lorentz on Film*), I remarked, among other things, that

> from the time you hear the band play "Dixie" until Claude Rains looks out the window as he says, "I wonder," *They Won't Forget* is as nerve-wracking a picture as you've ever seen, or will see for many a day. Not adapted, but built completely on Ward Greene's terse and bitter novel, "Death in the Deep South," Mervyn LeRoy's production is not only an honest picture, but an example of real movie making.

John had not seen the movie, but I told him enough about it so that he was looking forward to meeting the producer of his play. We made a date to see LeRoy at MGM and went out there at midday. We were greeted by the usual arrogant, snippy office people, who to begin with didn't know exactly where Mr. LeRoy's office was and gave us vague directions on how to find him in the new producers' building. We found the building, but it was getting near lunch time and many of the offices were vacant. We went into them, dialed the telephones, and left messages with anyone who answered. We picked up a phrase (that John and I used later on when it seemed appropriate) we overheard one man say to another: "This will make it much more magnificent or much worse."

We finally met LeRoy in his office, and after we said hello, LeRoy said brightly to John, "I'm going to change the character of Lenny!"

John glared at LeRoy with a Prussian menacing look and roared, "Why?"

End of interview with Mr. LeRoy. John just stood up and walked out, so I had to stand up and walk out with him.

That night with our drinks John ate about half a bushel of shrimp and a good dinner on top of that. The next morning he looked a little pale and told me he had been nauseated in the night, and it was because of our going to MGM. I think it may have been because of the shrimp, but he may have been right. It was a rude experience from beginning to end.

Our next visits were much happier ones, if not fruitful.

I had conceived of making *In Dubious Battle* with James Cagney and Paul Muni playing the leads, with John writing the script with me, and me directing in a location that would be, if not actually the lettuce fields of Salinas, a terrain similar to John's. I had conceived of the stars, John, and myself agreeing to work for minimum salaries for Warner Brothers (who owned Cagney and Muni), with all of us getting a percentage of the net profits. All during our efforts to get *In Dubious Battle* produced, neither John nor I had a contract with each other. Without discussing anything about money, we trusted each other, and John trusted his agents to look after him if we got down to business with anyone. I had the same trust of Misses Otis and Williams; furthermore, being employed by the U.S. government, I did not have an agent.

I called James Cagney and asked if he would meet with John and me for a business talk, and he as usual was courteous and invited us to his home in Coldwater Canyon in Beverly Hills. We were received in Jimmy's den, which contained a comfortable library with a comfortable leather couch and leather chairs, and we proceeded to reveal our proposition to him.

He contemplated the matter for a while, and then said, "If Muni will do it, I'll do it."

We explained that we had not approached Warner Brothers yet and had started with him with the hope that he would help us persuade Muni to work with us on our terms. Toward the end of our interview, I told Jim that there was one thing he might not like and that was, according to the novel, he would have to die off-screen.

Jim was a gifted mimic and a great storyteller, but he answered that revelation with the most extraordinary remark I ever heard him say during the many years we were acquainted. Glaring at me and red in the face, he bellowed, "I can OUT-ACT Muni off-screen!"

I do not recall any maneuvers on our part or any work done by any agents, but not long after our meeting with Cagney, we had an appointment at Warner Brothers with Bill Hawks, director Howard Hawks's brother. Bill was a pilot, I discovered later, and a very pleasant character who got down to business right away. He said Warner would give the two of us a joint contract for $4,500 a week, but that there were a couple of conditions: one was that we would not be able to go on location, and the other was that we would have an experienced producer, William Dieterle, in charge of us. Dieterle's credits up to that time were not impressive, but he had begun to produce fairly good movies for Warner, including: *A Midsummer Night's Dream* in 1935, *The Story of Louis Pasteur* in 1936, and *The Life of Emile Zola* in 1937 (the last film probably had just been released before our interview with Bill Hawks at Warner).

In any case, John and I both said we had to go on location, as it was an integral part of the work, and I said, from what I knew of Cagney's reports about playing in *A Midsummer Night's Dream*, he probably would object to working with Dieterle. For my part, I didn't want to have to have a German who directed by the signs of the zodiac and his horoscope (as Charles Laughton had told me Dieterle did) and who on the set was appareled in white gloves.

That was the end of our joint attempts to get someone to let us make *In Dubious Battle* our way. Both of us turned to other things after our efforts in Hollywood, but John occasionally in writing me would say, "*In Dubious Battle* is yours." Of course I never acknowledged that gift, as I didn't feel the book was optioned to me, and I'm sure neither did John's agents, but it was an extraordinary and generous gift John tried to give me.

Over the years in postwar times Cagney and I would go fishing in Martha's Vineyard each summer. We were part of Cagney's painting and fishing fraternity after we had our first boat built. Jim retold many anecdotes about me, most of them truthful, but the one he told often was the time he, Steinbeck, and I were having dinner at Chasen's, and

I got all wound up describing my concept of a sequence in the movie we were going to make from *In Dubious Battle*. John sat there quietly for a while and then interrupted me by saying, "Pare, would you mind breaking that down into words?"

Good ideas. Good times.

THE MAKING OF *THE FIGHT FOR LIFE*

In the spring of 1938 I was busy in New York and Washington following Tom Corcoran's suggestions for my finding a new home for my organization, which consisted of me, my devoted secretary, Elizabeth Roberts, and a few loyal employees from the Washington business and publicity offices. One proposition was that we could get money for production from some of the money being spent on World's Fair exhibits. This was bewildering, exhausting, and nonproductive.

Another proposition was that we should become part of the Fine Arts Division of the U.S. Treasury. The head of that division was a crippled man, a close friend of Roosevelt's, a former banker who had turned painter and who was one of the most amusing and honest men I met during my years of government service. His name was Ned Bruce. He was semiparalyzed on one side, and he carried a crutch which had a folding tray inside it with a place for a highball glass and a cigarette tray. I believe he was a classmate from the Harvard days of the president, but anyway, they had been friends for many years. Early in the New Deal he had reminded the president of the regulations passed under President Andrew Jackson which called for the Treasury Department to devote a percentage of the building costs of public buildings to sculptures and paintings and appropriate decorations. The president had made him head of the committee, and in turn Ned Bruce had chosen to form art committees whereby artists and sculptors would *themselves* hold competitions and choose the winning artists.

I was told I had to show my movies to Secretary of the Treasury Henry Morgenthau before Ned could consider taking me into his organization. The first meeting was cancelled just as I was on the way to the airport, and a second one was finally arranged in the auditorium either in Treasury or Commerce, and the secretary talked just as Mary Pickford had all through the showing of *The Plow That Broke the Plains*—not about the film, but about the Great Plains and the amount of money the government had devoted for relief for that area. "I have told Frank a dozen times that we should buy that place and put it out as a park because they are always having droughts and dust storms, and we are always having to put up relief money and it will never change out there, and we will go broke if we have to keep bailing them out."

Finally, looking pained after the film closed and saying he didn't have time to see *The River*, he remarked that he didn't know much about art, that in fact the only way he learned about artistic things was that Mrs. Morgenthau came in the bathroom and told him about art events while he was shaving.

I enjoyed my acquaintance with Mr. and Mrs. Bruce, but that didn't get me into his outfit.

: : :

I was given my directive establishing the U.S. Film Service and making me its chief on August 13, 1938. I made arrangements with my cameraman, Floyd Crosby, shortly afterward to meet me at Grand Coulee Dam, where we would take some pictures of it and the Columbia River gorge before our shooting the area for *Ecce Homo*.

I stopped on the way in San Francisco just to say hello to Steinbeck and Joseph Henry Jackson, and I took those studio recordings with me to play for them. Joe had, besides his column in the *San Francisco Chronicle*, a one-hour review talk show on Sundays at the National Broadcasting Company studio. He made arrangements with NBC for me to have the radio broadcast of "Ecce Homo" played at their recording studios, which were in the Palace Hotel, I think (if not the Palace, then the Fairmont, as it was one of the grand old establishments up in the Nob Hill area).

Both men seemed pleased with the work. This time, instead of John's Rendezvous, I went down to John's home to talk about work.

I presume it was the next day, which turned out to be one of those piercingly bright, hot California days in summer. My first recollection of that day was of Carol pouring herself a drink (I think a long gin drink) and then turning on a big record playing machine they had. I know it was Beethoven, and I think it was the Ninth Symphony she put on.

Meantime, John had started to open a bottle of red wine for us, and either he broke the corkscrew or he couldn't work it, so he took the wine in to his workbench and put the bottle in a vise and horsed around with extraordinarily unsuccessful attempts to use his tools to get the cork out of the bottle.

Meantime, Carol turned up the volume on the record player to an intolerable decibel level, so we could not hear a word we said to each other. We continued to be dry and deafened.

I presume John hollered at Carol to turn down the machine. After some embarrassing dialogue between John and Carol, she suddenly took off and started running down a rather steep hill alongside John's house. He continued to fiddle with the wine with the vise when we heard screams. I said to John that Carol had fallen down and hurt herself. He dismissed it for a while, but I insisted he go tend to his wife. He carried her up the hill and took her to the bedroom and reported that she only had a sprained ankle.

Suddenly, in the midst of this domestic crisis, John said, "Let's go call on Chaplin. He's down on the peninsula."

He obviously had Chaplin's telephone number on hand, and after a short conversation in the bedroom with Carol, we took off, I having to explain to John that I had to fly to Portland that afternoon and that I had a reservation on a one-engine little puddle-jumper which would connect me with a flight taking me to Portland. He assured me that would all be possible, so we drove to, I think, Pebble Beach. Anyway, it was some kind of development of new little attached houses with a sweeping view of the ocean. Some of the land evidently had belonged to John's father, and his sister, Beth, was married and lived near where Chaplin was hiding.

I gathered from John's casual explanation that Chaplin didn't wish at the moment to talk to the Internal Revenue Service—a technical problem that bothered a great many Hollywood stars.

Chaplin greeted us effusively enough. He was wearing a very stylish English felt hat. He walked us into the living room, which was the most barren, empty, spic-and-span room I ever entered. There was a working fireplace with logs in it, but other than that there was not a magazine, a book, an ashtray, or any other sign of human activities in the area. No sooner had we greeted each other than the telephone started ringing. It was not a bell, it was the rattle-type signal, and it w-h-i-r-r-e-d and w-h-i-r-r-e-d for minutes, sounding like a very agitated rattlesnake. Finally, after the noise stopped temporarily, Chaplin turned to us and said, "That's Sam Goldwyn calling, and he wants to buy my interest in United Artists. I don't want to talk to him—I don't trust the son-of-a-bitch."

He then related a long story of an incident that had happened years before, during silent movie days. He said Goldwyn came into his studio unannounced and sat down and told Chaplin he wanted to borrow a hundred thousand dollars. He promised to pay it back with interest in thirty days. He said he needed that amount of money to finish the picture he was making. He then added that he also was in love with Mabel Normand, and then he started to cry. Finally, Chaplin said, "I gave him the money."

He reflected for a moment and then said, "He paid me back in thirty days with interest."

The phone started w-h-i-r-r-i-n-g again, and Chaplin shouted over the noise, "I just don't trust that son-of-a-bitch!"

I remember very little else about that visit except that Chaplin kept trying to make a fire in the fireplace in order to grill what looked like the hindquarters of a prize-winning black angus steer. He then brought out a bottle of Chambertin wine (which he had success in opening), and we each had a glass. By then, it was getting close to time for me to leave to catch my little puddle-jumper to Portland, but John wanted me to meet his sister.

It turned out that it was not much of a walk to her house. She was a big, comfortable-looking woman and stood on her steps inviting us over and over into her house, but John said no, that we were in a hurry. So we passed the time of day with that big, pleasant woman named Beth and then went back to Chaplin's.

Chaplin sent for his Rolls Royce and chauffeur and drove me to the little airport either in Monterey or Pebble Beach. They followed me to the gate, John waving a bottle of that fine wine, and both of them shouting, "Government clerk! Government clerk!" trying to get me to stay overnight with them.

In his journal, John remarks under August 23, 1938:

Pare came over the weekend. Big time. Carol sprained her ankle q.t. Went down to the peninsula with Pare and spent the night at Chaplin's place. Talked all night. Of course I lost a day of work. I am afraid Pare doesn't need me on this job and I think he knows it but hasn't admitted it yet. I'll work if I am needed. . . . Pare made me feel much better about the country at large. But I am very much confused.

Perhaps this is as good a place as any to discuss the title *The Grapes of Wrath*. I had, as I reported earlier, played the records of "Ecce Homo" for John and Joe Jackson. I had asked Bill Robson to make sure that I could talk with the talented composer-conductor Bernard Herrmann, staff musician at CBS, about the concluding music of "Ecce Homo."

I once spoke with an old riot policeman, who said, "If you hear a mob approaching you singing and hollering and carrying slogans, don't be frightened, because all they want to do is make a loud noise and call attention to themselves. Now if you hear the sound of footsteps approaching slowly without a single sound emanating from the crowd, call for reinforcements. They mean business."

I asked Robson if, instead of a triumphant tempo or a jolly revival meeting beat, that the opening verse and chorus of the "Battle Hymn of the Republic" be sung with an ominous battle tempo, along with asking the sound men to increase the volume slowly instead of the tempo. They did just what I asked. It made for a very spine-chilling sound to me.

It could be John remembered my emphasis on this conclusion after he had heard the radio show of "Ecce Homo" with Joe Jackson and me in San Francisco. The words of that verse and chorus are:

Mine eyes have seen the glory of the coming of the Lord.

He is trampling out the vintage where *the grapes of wrath* are
    stored.

He hath loosed the fateful lightning of his terrible swift sword.

His truth is marching on.

Glory! Glory! Hallelujah!
Glory! Glory! Hallelujah!
Glory! Glory! Hallelujah!
His truth is marching on.

Sometime after the broadcast on May 21, 1938, I had regular records made from the big studio cuttings, and I am sure I sent an album of them to John, as I have a letter from him forwarded to me in Cleveland, where I started on my first industrial location for the movie version of *Ecce Homo* at the White Motor Works. In that letter John thanks me for the records. I am sure they were an album of "Ecce Homo" records, and I am pretty sure that is where Carol Steinbeck got her idea for the title *The Grapes of Wrath.*

As John became so enthusiastic about the title, he wrote his publisher that he wished to reproduce the whole score and complete words of "The Battle Hymn of the Republic" as a conclusion to *The Grapes of Wrath.*

In all our acquaintance, John was more than generous to me, so if I was instrumental in his finding a great title for his book, I'm delighted, but I do not wish any public credit. The novel would have been internationally famous no matter what the title.

The rest of the letter from John, dated January 23, 1939, is newsworthy enough so that I put it here verbatim:

Mr. Pare Lorentz (Personal, please forward)
Original address crossed out and readdressed to:
Cleveland Hotel
Cleveland, Ohio

Dear Pare:

I haven't any idea when or whether this will reach you. The records came and they are very fine. Thank you. It is the largest album I ever saw. We went south after Christmas, saw Chaplin and Vidor (who thinks you are about due out here). Picked up Elizabeth Otis and brought her back up here. About a month ago a nerve in my leg started acting up. It was diagnosed as sciatica. Got worse and worse until last week I had a complete physical and found that metabolism was dangerously low. Means I have to stay in bed two weeks ($1\frac{1}{2}$ now) and take thyroid and vitamins. Seems that I worked too hard on my book and just worked myself out and very near a nervous collapse. But I'll be all right in ten days.

I want to get in touch with you. In the first place I'm all ready to go to work if you still want me to or will be in ten days. And in the second, I'd like to discuss with you the picture Milestone plans to make of M & M and in the third place, not in importance, we'd like to see you. So do let me hear from you.

We thought we were going to New York this winter but didn't have to finally. We're glad because I felt so lousy.

Finished my book before Christmas and except for galleys am all through. I think it is pretty good technically. I hope so.

But if I could be of any service in your work, I'd like to be. I am quite selfish about this. I want to learn the medium or something about it and I want to study it under you. That's honest enough anyway. If in return I can do dialogue or anything I'll be glad. But do let me hear.

Charlie is really going ahead with the picture. Started luring designers and ordering sets. Dan is sort of keeping him company, I think, and Dan is a good boy.

It's a little hard to write in bed. In answering—unless you aren't in a hurry—wire because we only get our mail when someone comes up and that may not be for a week. With me down, we're marooned somewhat.

John

Subsequently, I have—for him—a long letter which was the most professional letter I ever had from John. He had many ideas for me, including my putting an agriculture sequence in *Ecce Homo* and also asking me to introduce him to Secretary Wallace, and he told me he would send me photographs. I have no recollection of his doing that.

I did sometime or another in our acquaintance tell him about the poignant photographs Dorothea Lange had sent to the Resettlement Administration and how she helped me gather a group of migrants in the camp outside Bakersfield. Professor Paul Taylor, sometime after Dorothea died, told me John had written a postal card to Dorothea, but I don't know whether she sent him photographs later or what he said or what Dorothea did for him, if anything.

John was really fired up after this trip and wrote to me lucidly, but with both fists:

March 6
Los Gatos
California

Dear Pare:

I just got back from another week in the field where the starvation and illness have been driven to a fine logical conclusion by the wet and flood. It might interest you to know but not to repeat just now that a nice revolutionary feeling is the concommitant of this suffering. I mean it is something that I hoped but was not sure of, that a certain amount of suffering is deadening but a quick increase such as this storm shakes off the apathy. The thing is very dangerous now. I have many things to tell you.

In the matter of crops, there is beet thinning coming up and then pea picking, both of them stoop crops. A machine has been invented and it is being manufactured in Fresno that will stop all the cotton chopping—one of the main sources of employment in the spring. It is not an expensive gadget and one man and a light tractor pulling it across the fields will thin and weed and ditch the cotton fields all in one operation and the opposite of the Rust brothers are backing it. I am doing a series for Life. Went down with a photographer and we got magnificent pictures of people.

It may be too tough for Life but I will send you a file of the pictures for your own edification and also for giving you an idea of the appearance of the people. Words and generalities don't mean anything anymore, but I hope with these pictures to pin a badge of shame on the greedy sons of bitches who are causing this condition and it is definitely caused, make no mistake about that. I know that name calling won't do anything but they are touchy about the tourist who might not come to California to spend his money because he might see such suffering. That is the only good this might do, and that is why I am doing it.

Of course the industrial picture is necessary but it seems to me that some work on farm labor might cement these two forces. The Associated Farmers are advertising all over the country that we pay our farm labor the highest wages in the world. This brings new droves. In the first pea picking when the peas are thin and expensive and desirable, a man at thirty cents a basket, may make thirty cents a day and he may not. He may have to crawl to a dozen vines before he finds a single pod. We're going to have a wage cut and a cut in the piece work level. There will be bloodshed this spring and summer, lots of it.

I plan to send you some pictures of the Salinas and Stockton strike where people were murdered in cold blood. I would like to see Wallace very much if he cares to see me. I would like to find out what the true attitude of his department is. People in its ranks out here are sabotaging the work right and left and drawing salaries from the Associated Farmers for so doing. The black list is working under state relief and that is a beautiful thing.

It works like this. Anyone who is getting state relief must put his name on a list at the local chamber of commerce so that if employment comes up he will be available. And in the chambers of commerce the black listing is done. If a man has so much as been reported as saying he favored organization, he is listed and within a week or so some reason is found for removing him from the relief rolls. It is such a dirty thing out here that if I keep from getting shot while taking a few choice sadists with me in this year, I shall have used forbearance which is remarkable.

I think that is all or if it isn't, it is all I can think of right now.

It was so good to have you out here.

Bye,
John

All during the time John was working on *The Grapes of Wrath*, the summer and fall of 1938, and was fretting about not hearing from me or not having any plans for work from me—which is noted in his journal—I was pretty well overwhelmed with a combination of administrative duties and arrangements for photographing industrial America, particularly an automobile assembly plant.

Meanwhile, there was a sudden change in my priorities because of the lack of continuing funds for *Ecce Homo* and the promise of funding for a new project.

I cannot remember the date, but I do remember the time and place. My film editor, Lloyd Nosler, and I were in the cutting room at Sam Goldwyn's studios, examining prints and out-takes of *The River*, when someone delivered a telegram to me. It was from Dr. Paul de Kruif. I had never met the man, but I had read his book *Microbe Hunters* and enjoyed it very much. His wire said in effect, "Just finished seeing 'The River' and 'The Plow That Broke the Plains.' I hereby give you the dramatic rights to all my books. Hope we can meet in New York City."

I was bewildered, but Lloyd was delighted and felt I should hurry up and meet the man. That transpired in New York City in the apartment of George Woods. I had known George slightly at our club, the Players. He was a quiet man who was working then for Chase Bank. Later he became chief executive officer of the First Boston Corporation, and from there he was elected president of the United Nations World Bank. I imagine he had been quietly an angel, helping finance some Broadway plays, and I imagine one of them had been *Yellow Jack*, which was dramatized by

Sidney Howard from de Kruif's account of Dr. Walter Reed's fight against yellow fever. In any case, he was an old friend of de Kruif's who brought with him to our first meeting Surgeon General Dr. Thomas Parran.

Dr. Parran said that the president was planning on sending a message to Congress sometime in the spring of 1939 in which he would ask for a large sum of money for a campaign to cure or prevent five diseases: infantile paralysis, syphilis, smallpox, malaria, and tuberculosis. Dr. Parran was engaged in establishing a nationwide program of blood testing for syphilis, including sending "bloodmobiles" into rural areas; also he had written a book about syphilis called *Shadow on the Land* and had been responsible for breaking the taboo that existed prior to his becoming surgeon general which caused newspapers and magazines to avoid using generic names of venereal diseases—weaseling out by referring to them as "social diseases."

I had been deeply moved by a section in de Kruif's most recent book *The Fight for Life*, in which he described the Chicago Maternity Center, which had been established before the turn of the century by Dr. Joseph B. De Lee in the heart of the Chicago slums.

De Lee had been a student in the hospital in Vienna where Dr. Ignaz Semmelweis became the first doctor ever to use *cleanliness* as a treatment for child-bed fever. In Paul's book he writes:

> Ignaz Semmelweis was becoming enthusiastic, obsessed, and a nuisance to his fellow doctors by a terrific scrubbing of his hands, a persnickety cleaning of his finger nails, a washing of the very scent of death off his hands, a making of quadruple sure by an epic soaking of his hands in strong chlorine water—
>
> Before those hands touched the inside of any mother wounded during the coming of her baby.

Dr. Semmelweis died in a madhouse in Vienna, but by then Dr. De Lee had put up a sign in his little clinic in the Chicago slums advertising free prenatal care and eventually was training interns sent to him by surrounding medical schools.

Reluctantly, Dr. Parran agreed with me that if we were going to make medical movies, it would be sensible to start with the beginning of life itself. Therefore, we would show how Dr. De Lee had a better mortality record than many hospitals did.

It took me some time to discover why Dr. Parran seemed somewhat sad at my choosing maternal and infant welfare as a first medical motion picture. It turned out that the U.S. government control over maternal and infant welfare was assigned to the Department of Labor. Therefore, idiotically enough, the U.S. Public Health Service had no responsibility for women's and infants' health. Even so, Dr. Parran was a staunch friend and advisor during the making of *The Fight for Life*.

: : :

I remember vividly the last scene I shot for *The Fight for Life* for many reasons. My next-door neighbor in the Garden of Allah was, as I stated before, Dudley Digges, the great Irish character actor. He was playing a major part in *Raffles* for Sam Goldwyn when I asked him to play the old doctor for me. He refused over and over, not because of money, as he was getting a tidy sum from Goldwyn, but I think because he was worried about being in a, to him, amateur film. Finally he agreed when I told him I could find no one suitable in Hollywood. One of the things that tickled him was when I asked him one time how come he had a broken nose. He said he was playing a lead part in the play *Disraeli*, with George Arliss in the lead, and the First World War had just started. When they played in Denver some British stagehand had put up a notice for the actors to please contribute to the Prince of Wales Ambulance Fund. All the actors did except Dudley, whereupon the stagehand bopped him one and broke his nose.

I told him I wanted to shoot him a profile showing the broken nose from what had, in other movies, been his "bad" side. Most surgeons I had met during research and interviews for *The Fight for Life* had been boxers, football players, or skiers or had engaged in some contact or strenuous sport, and many of them had disfigured noses and ears to show for it. I told him a broken nose would lend more authority to his character.

It was the beginning of the usual Hollywood September heat wave. I had figured we were going to have a tough day. All morning he blew up, and I quickly saw why—he had no one to play with and to answer back. He had to hit his own pauses and emphasis for three minutes while McCormick just sat and stared at him. I had ordered two off-white French flannel shirts for him to wear under his white coat. Sure enough, by noon he had sweat through the first shirt and it did please him that I had a new clean one ready for him.

We went on and on that afternoon, and he would never quite finish his lines without stuttering and cursing in general, saying things like, "I'm too old," or "Get somebody else, you don't need me to do this for you," and so forth. Floyd Crosby came up with the wittiest remark he ever made during our long acquaintance late in the afternoon when we had to set up again after Dudley had goofed. Floyd turned to the crew and said, "Gentlemen, you are going to have to learn medicine the hard way." That is a line from the medical lecture given the students at the Chicago Maternity Center which we had already shot in the studio. I think it helped Dudley, that and his wonderful old heart. He put his glasses down and thought a minute and we shot one. There was no stutter, no hesitation or lack of authority from beginning to end. We were all quite literally and figuratively breathless.

When we got home we turned on the radio. It was September 2. Hitler had invaded Poland and bombed Warsaw the day before. No sooner had we heard the news start than it was interrupted by the tired, thin voice of Neville Chamberlain, saying, "His Majesty's government is in a state of war with the Chancellor of Germany." We turned off the radio and Dudley, who had been involved in the Irish troubles way back during the First World War, smiled wickedly, if sadly, and said: "And now the British are going to get it."

Paul de Kruif had warned me over the telephone while I was working in Detroit that the U.S. government was no longer interested in internal affairs much less in maternal and infant welfare. The prime minister's declaration convinced me Paul was right.

Some film professors and historians in the United States refuse to include *The Fight for Life* in any list of documentary films on the grounds that I employed actors and actresses. Except for the three leading men, all the "actors" and "actresses" shown in the actual Chicago Maternity Center were patients of the center, nurses of the center, and interns working at the center. The locations, save for the final sequence, were the Maternity Center, Dr. De Lee's own operating rooms in Lying In Hospital, and homes of patients of the center, and finally, former or current patients, in their own homes.

I selected the cast for one sequence—the hemorrhage sequence—in Hollywood. The basic examinations of patients in Chicago were with patients who showed tendencies that might have led them to come down with one of the three causes of death in maternal cases.

Prior to these examinations, which were all shot silently in Chicago but with the actors speaking their lines, which we then synchronized and dubbed in in Hollywood, the whole movie had three soliloquies and one long uninterrupted lecture by Dudley Digges, and except for the last sequence all medical work was done silently but was, as I have said, dubbed in later. Because of my skilled soundmen from the Sam Goldwyn Studio and the disciplined crew of actors and actresses, the picture is unrevealing as to those technical methods.

The medical lecture given by actor Storrs Haynes, playing the head of the center, sets forth the sequences that will follow:

> We have two objectives here at the Center—to bring modern obstetrical care to the poor women of the city, and to teach you the art and science of obstetrics as practised by the best institutions in the country. (*A series of portraits of pregnant women is seen, and then Ballou is picked out again.*) As doctors, we have to face this fact: today, almost as many mothers die bringing children into the world, as did twenty-five years ago. With all the new science and medicine we have in this country, we lose more human lives from childbearing, than we do from cancer. The deaths of mothers and infants under one month ranks second only to heart disease in the total mortality figures.
>
> You know the three things that kill mothers. Eclampsia, infection, hemorrhage. And of these, child-bed fever—infection at birth—is still the chief killer. Thirty-five out of one hundred women who die, die from infection. And most of them could have been saved.

Back to John. Early in April I came home from Detroit, where we had finished photographing the Plymouth automobile straight line, and began preparations for making *The Fight for Life*. Out of the blue I received a complete set of galleys of *The Grapes of Wrath* with no note or anything from John with it. My letter of April 6, John's undated letter from Los Gatos, my communication of April 10, and John's agreement are self-explanatory, and I include them here without any unnecessary comment:

April 6, 1939

Dear John:

My whole house was upset for two days while I was reading your book, both aloud and to myself, and I was very excited but perfectly sober when I called you.

I read in the paper that you were, yourself, putting on "Of Mice and Men" in Los Angeles, and as I know you will be greeted with business from all over the country as soon as your book comes out I am quite serious in not wishing to ask you to leave until you yourself want to very much.

I think of many passages in your book all the time and it is a fine feeling to have been with you and to know what a wonderful job you have done.

There is nothing but reaction and war in this part of the country and it is hard for us to work. A wire to this office at any time from you will find me as I start west, and you can travel and start on the payroll any day you wish.

I should imagine Carol is very happy that the book is finished and that she kept people away from you so you could do it. We are homesick for the people we like in the west and I will be glad to get there.

Yours,
Pare Lorentz

Los Gatos, California

Dear Pare:

It was very good to hear from you the other night. I hope the reaction is not going to be as thick as you suppose. But apart from that I should like to join you soon. I had thought of leaving here sometime about the sixteenth or seventeenth. Where could I meet you about then? I'll leave by train and then later take what planes I need. Carol has such a ghastly fear of planes that I wouldn't put her to the apprehension of knowing that I was going out by plane. But what I want to know is this. Starting by train about the sixteenth or seventeenth where and when shall I meet you? I do not want any of the mess you mention. I had a little in New York two summers ago and I think I won't even let it start this time. Actually I shall technically be gone from here on the fourteenth. Carol will so state over the phone. Do let me know these things as soon as you can.

It is beautiful here now and I am torn but I want to work with you and this will be waiting for me when I get back. The trees are in blossom and the green grass is high. But the heat has been on for some time. The Ass farmers have been smearing me up and down the state to try to kill this book in advance. Their idea of a smear is to claim and so to write that I am a bosom friend of Harry Bridges, the antichrist. I unfortunately do not know him but I would like to. I admire him as an honest and effective man.

Well, there it is. I'll be looking for some kind of communication from you soon. It was very difficult to hear you the other night. I expect that the other four parties on our line were listening and that cuts down the power.

I am awfully glad you like the new book. It seems to be selling rather wildly even before the publication date. I hope it gets quite a bit of circulation.

So long and do let me hear from you soon.

John

April 10, 1939

Mr. John Steinbeck
Los Gatos, California

Dear Mr. Steinbeck:

Mr. Lorentz was just on the wire. He asked me to read him your letter and to transmit to you the following information:

1. He expects to be in Chicago April 25. He is sending to you government transportation requests to cover your trip, and unless he wires you to the contrary, wants you to come to the Morrison Hotel on that date.

2. He is engaged in casting, finishing the script and arranging for sets for a three-reel picture "The Fight For Life."

3. You can, if you will, help locate tenements, criticize the script and look at footage already existing on "The Fight For Life."

4. Mr. Lorentz expects to have a large crew, and not much time to do much talking as he would like. However, he believes that you and he can talk on the way west. It is possible that you and he may do some work on "Ecce Homo."

It is probably unnecessary to reiterate that Mr. Lorentz is delighted that you are going to work with him but he wanted me to state it once more.

Mr. John S. Bridgeman, who handles all matters of finance, travel, etc., is enclosing a letter and travel requests with this. If there is anything either of us can do to help clarify the situation or to answer any of your questions, please do not hesitate to let us know.

Sincerely yours,
Miriam Bell,
Assistant to Mr. Lorentz

Los Gatos
April 13, 1939

Dear Pare:

I'll be there on the 25th. I'll probably start a day early and see an uncle of mine who lives in Chicago. If you hear that I am east, it's because Paul tells people who call up, and a hell of a lot of them are doing it, that I have gone east on business. It saves me from having to talk to people. I hope I get away with it.

I guess that's all. See you on the 25th. If you have a change of plans or place, wire me before the 21st.

So long,
John

John was very inconspicuous during my working days in Chicago. I know that being a practical soul, he had Carol examined by Dr. Beatrice Tucker, codirector of the center, to find out whether she was able to bear children. I do not know anything about the result, and I do not know whether it led to the final breakup of John and Carol. John never talked about it and I never asked him anything about it. Another reason I didn't see much of John was that he kept himself with the electricians and grips and I never remember seeing him near the shooting inside the center or inside the slum houses of the patients.

Paul de Kruif came over from his home, Wake Robin, on the shores of Lake Michigan in the Dutch town of Holland. He and John got along fine. They both were large-sized men. (I know de Kruif wore a size nineteen shirt collar. I never did ask him about his shoe size.) John was a big-boned, large man.

Shortly before he died, the great Neapolitan actor-director Vittorio de Sica gave an interview to an American reporter in which he stated that he never would go to Hollywood to make a movie. He added that if he ever went to an American city to make a movie it would be Chicago. At the time, after I read that, I was tempted to write him a letter saying, "Dear Signor de Sica: About your going to Chicago to make a movie . . . forget it."

Another reason I didn't see much of John is that I was beset by some serious production problems which had nothing to do with movie making itself. To put my production problems in chronological order, they were:

1. My life and the lives of my photographic crew were threatened by the walking delegate of the cameramen and projectionists' union.

2. After finishing shooting one night in a Polish stockyard worker's home with a wonderful pregnant woman and a wonderful child, we were threatened by a mob of half-drunk, completely surly Polish gentlemen led by the husband of the pregnant wife who threatened to break our camera and then demanded fifty thousand dollars as permission for us to use this three days of film we had shot of his wife and his abject home. He was unemployed, he said, but nevertheless public exposure of his terrible poverty would damage the lives of his family and himself and he could only allow it for fifty thousand dollars.

3. Finally, Warner Brothers, having failed to purchase the rights to de Kruif's book in order to star Bette Davis and Paul Muni as codirectors of the Chicago Maternity Center, resorted to bribery right on the spot through their representative in Chicago.

I'll discuss the problems in that order.

We had not been working more than a few days when I had an unannounced visit at my hotel room by the walking delegate of the cameramen and projectionists' union. He informed me that I had to either employ the Chicago cameramen's union men or pay them wages for each technician I was employing.

I showed him my credentials: letters from the surgeon general of the United States, my U.S. government employment card as head of the U.S. film service, a letter from Dr. Joseph B. De Lee, and so on. He said he would report my position to his local and would be checking with me again. (I remember his looks and his name vividly, but I'm not about to report either one, as he may have a grandson, and if he does, he'll be armed.)

The next day I was working in the Maternity Center when I was called to the telephone, and my friend from the union said that if I didn't abide by their rules, he couldn't speak for the lives of me and my crew.

I was so outraged, I rode off in all directions. First, properly, I called my superior, Lowell Mellett, at the National Emergency Council. I felt he would be sympathetic to my problem, as his brother, who was a newspaper editor for Scripps Howard in Canton, Ohio, had been murdered by gangsters as he sat at his desk because of having exposed the mob in his newspaper. I was wrong. The first thing Lowell did was to holler at me not to let the press know I was having any problems because Colonel McCormick would make a big thing of it in the *Chicago Tribune*. I asked politely if it was better for me to get shot than to have the press uninformed. I then sent wires to some lawyers I knew who represented the motion picture industry, and I felt it only fair to tell my camera crew about our problems.

William Clothier had been hired by Crosby as his operating camera-man. Bill had just returned from covering the Spanish Civil War for a newsreel company. (After he worked for me I wanted him to join my Air Transport Command Movie Unit, but he already had promised General Spaatz he would join the Eighth Air Force Combat Camera-men's Unit, during which time he did most of the combat flying photography in the great movie *Memphis Belle*.) It happened that Bill was president of his cameramen's local union in Hollywood, so he called and asked for help. He was told that they knew about the Chicago union and that nothing could be done about them, and so they advised, "Be careful!"

I also had been advised to call upon a man named Gael Sullivan, executive secretary to Mayor Kelley. Gael was an extraordinarily hand-some Irishman with the childish robin's-egg-blue innocent eyes of

Irish horse dealers, as described by James Cagney after he returned from his first trip to Ireland. Gael said that the year before, Mayor Kelley had employed an independent movie company to do a campaign movie about himself. Some Chicago union friends said if they went through with this project, they'd kill the mayor. Instead of going ahead with the movie, they canceled it entirely.

Gael moved up fairly rapidly in the Democratic party ranks. He became secretary to the postmaster general and later became executive secretary of the Democratic National Committee. The last thing he did was to become president of the Independent Motion Picture Theater Owners of America, and I saw him several times during that period. He always had good, sound ideas, and he also was favorably inclined towards my activities. He had a pleasant, sensible, good wife, and he helped good causes during his times of political influence.

I finally wired some lawyers who represented banks who owned movie stock, reminding them of some unreported scandals, and at last I called Steve Early at the White House and told him that I wanted some help to keep from getting killed when I was working as a government employee.

Meantime Floyd Crosby told me that he had been unable to rent a generator and some floodlights, which we needed for photographing the scene that opens *The Fight for Life*—the night shot and a long pan of the facade of the entrance to Lying In Hospital from which we cut to the birth of the baby and the death of the mother.

The night after I called the White House, I had two other unannounced visitors. One was a sprightly little fellow with grey white hair and sparkling eyes whose name was Judge George E. Q. Johnson. He had with him a courtly but extremely young man who had just graduated from the University of Virginia Law School and who had just entered into the service of the FBI. They listened quietly while I told them my story and showed them my credentials and told them about the movie and the reasons for it. When I got to the part about the generator and the lights and told them about the suppliers who had told Crosby they didn't dare rent us any equipment, as they would get their stores blown up, they became quite interested.

Finally the Judge told me to write a registered letter to one of the supply houses and keep a carbon copy and give it to them and to go about my business. I did this the next morning and the morning following I was again interrupted at the Chicago Maternity Center by my friend, the walking delegate. In an oozingly pleasant voice, he said, "We didn't know you were working for the government. Now is there anything we can *give* you? What kind of a generator do you want us to *give* you?"

I explained that we wanted to pay for our equipment, but he begged me to accept a gift from the union. So the Judge and his friend, the boy, had called on somebody about something. Anyway, that's the last we heard of them, and that's the way we worked in Chicago.

Number two almost did me in. Fortunately Paul de Kruif was in town with Dr. Wegner, the head of the venereal disease section of the U.S. Public Health Service. As I reported earlier, the service was doing a national blood test for syphilis, this action being run by Dr. Wegner. De Kruif was interested in his experiment.

I remember there was a big joke going around about the man who walked into a prophylactic dispensary that had been established by some foundation in Chicago and said to the attending nurse, "I'd like some syphilis." After some pleading with the gentleman, they finally got the reason for his weird request. He said: "The *Chicago Tribune* is against syphilis and I'm *for* anything Colonel McCormick is against."

The gallant husband of the pregnant woman we had photographed in her home had, as I said, demanded either we destroy the film we had taken of his wife at his home or we pay fifty thousand dollars. His buddies looked like a group that could come and get the film and destroy it without any trouble, so I was half crazy with anger that we might have to lose three days of wonderful footage. I didn't have the money or the time to find another pregnant woman as gracious and hardworking as the one we had been working with.

Dr. Wegner came over to my hotel and listened to the tale and said he would call up Dr. X, who was a very prominent urologist in Chicago and who had prominent men as patients. This was Saturday. Dr. Wegner and this famous doctor arranged for a meeting with my injured husband. Evidently it went on for several hours in a Polish barbershop.

Dr. Wegner came back to my hotel around dinnertime and told me rather dramatically I could keep the film and go about my business and there would be no legal action or any other kind of action taken against me. With the help of his friends, the Chicago police had discovered that the Polish gentleman had been absent from his home while we were working there because he was still finishing time in Joliet Prison, where he had spent five years as a fence for receiving stolen property.

I figured the reason he had put up this blackmail scheme in the first place was because Crosby had rented our camera from Grand National Studios and they had painted their name in big white letters on the film cases, so no matter what we said, our Polish friend felt we were a Hollywood outfit. It was not only scary but also a very low moment in our times in Chicago.

Concerning the third problem, as I reported earlier, Warner Brothers, having heard about my proposed movie based on Paul's book, had offered the publishers, Harcourt and Brace, fifty thousand dollars for the dramatic rights to the book. Don Brace was one of the most generous, charming, and decent men I ever encountered in the publishing business.

Brace said at the very beginning that Paul had given the rights to the U.S. government, with the condition that I make the movie, but with no price tag; that they had had enough things stolen from Paul by Hollywood outfits; and that they wouldn't mind his giving *The Fight for Life* away.

One of the things they said was that Warner Brothers had produced a movie, *Dr. Ehrlich's Magic Bullet,* which was written by John Huston, who had lived with Paul de Kruif in his home and had discussed the life of Dr. Ehrlich with him. Paul had shown Huston letters from Ehrlich which he kept in his safe. Warner Brothers paid no money to Paul whatsoever for the information he provided Huston for the movie *Dr. Ehrlich's Magic Bullet.* (In de Kruif's book *The Microbe Hunters,* chapter 12 is entitled "The Magic Bullet," and it is about Dr. Ehrlich's work.) This irked the hell out of both Brace and Harcourt, so they were against selling anything to Warner Brothers. Nevertheless, Warner Brothers didn't quit.

Paul and Howard Hunter, second in command of the Work Projects Administration, were great friends. Paul was interested in many public health and welfare projects, most of which he did in order to write about them and thus make some money, but as to the projects themselves, I know of none of them from which he asked any recompense himself. (Among other activities to which de Kruif devoted much of his time were those he performed in unpaid service as secretary of the President's Commission for Infantile Paralysis Research, the March of Dimes outfit.)

It happened that there was a federal or a government grant to the

Chicago Maternity Center pending in the governor's office, and Howard Hunter had some federal part of this grant endowment. He was in Chicago with Paul, and the word had come down from the governor's office that the center would get one hundred thousand dollars. That same evening we had been asked to meet with the Warner Brothers representative in Chicago. I think he was a booker or a salesman or a public relations man, but anyway he called and said he was speaking for Jack Warner personally. That was one of the merriest nights I had in an unmerry interlude.

We sat there in our rooms at the Drake Hotel drinking scotch while Jack Warner's representative (whose name was Sam something-or-other) said how much Jack loved the Chicago Maternity Center. He said he thought they needed a new automobile, and he was willing to buy one and give it to the center if they in turn would let Warner make the movie with Bette Davis and Paul Muni based, of course, on the writings of Dr. de Kruif. Like a wounded walrus, de Kruif rose up in the chair when he heard this offer and said that the doctors and nurses would *die* in a car given to the center by Jack Warner!

I think Dr. Tucker and Dr. Benaron were a little sad that they hadn't somehow squeezed a new car out of Warner Brothers, but they couldn't complain much to the man who helped them get one hundred thousand dollars.

So much for poor Sam. We laughed far into the night when he left.

:   :   :

John Steinbeck was either away with de Kruif or busy with my technicians, but I know I didn't ask him for help in solving these problems, as I felt my government should support and protect me. Later, when we got to Hollywood and had a final disaster facing us, John was of more help than I realized at the time.

When we finally went to Hollywood I put John up with me in my bungalow at the Garden of Allah in Beverly Hills, a famous hostelry which has long since been torn down for some high-rise establishment. My neighbors the first time I stayed there included Dudley and Mary Digges, Robert Benchley and Muggsy, and Charles Laughton and his wife Elsa Lanchester.

The very first evening after introducing John and Carol to Mr. Benchley and Muggsy, I was awakened several times by the sounds of marching, singing, and general merriment coming from the Benchley household. When I got up and started out the door for breakfast, John and Carol were just slowly exiting Mr. Benchley's welcoming party.

The minute we arrived at the Garden of Allah, there were a half-dozen messages waiting for John from people such as Charlie Chaplin and Spencer Tracy. I had registered John under a false name, but it didn't prevent people who wanted to work in his movies or wanted to see him about something or other from finding out where he was. John tried to stall them all off, but finally I asked him to leave, as I had sent word that I wished Dr. Benaron, codirector of the Chicago Maternity Center, to come out and help me with the final writing, in which I needed medical terminology and exact descriptions of a hemorrhage patient and what she would look like and what they would do and how they would do it in their efforts to save her life. John had become well-to-do and famous during our acquaintance and I couldn't work very well with the phone ringing for him every hour of the day.

John went over to a sort of stained-glass fleabag called the Aloha where my technicians were staying. Before he left he casually told me two things: first, that his agent had sold *The Grapes of Wrath* for seventy-five thousand dollars, which was quite a nice sum in those days of 1939. He told me also that he had script approval, and I jumped on him and said that Twentieth Century–Fox had more money in the bank than he did and they had much tougher lawyers, and the best thing he could do would be to request the best writing-directing team Twentieth Century could provide. He asked me whom I would suggest, and I told him Nunnally Johnson as his writer and John Ford as his director. Those were the two men Daryl F. Zanuck chose, but I do not know whether John asked his agent to tell Zanuck of his choice or whether he told Zanuck personally or how this happy combination came about.

Nunnally Johnson was an old friend, and he, upon getting the assignment to dramatize *The Grapes of Wrath*, made the public statement that "I feel like I am carrying the Holy Grail." Not only was he a friend, but he also was probably the most talented and disciplined writer that Zanuck had working for him. Also, he was about the only one Zanuck did not dare demean by cursing him out for having opinions while they were examining footage in the projection room or by making him accompany the great little king outdoors while he relieved himself or other such unpleasant royal demands.

Nunnally had been born in Columbus, Georgia, and was a first-class reporter who began writing humorous pieces for the old *Smart Set* while he was working on the *Brooklyn Eagle*. He had been an infantryman in the First World War, and besides being genuinely witty was quite a tough character. After the book and play of *Tobacco Road* came out, he was asked if he had known people like that in his home state of Georgia. Johnson replied, "Where I come from, we called people like that 'The Country Club' set." As I knew they would, John and Nunnally got along very well together.

In the rave review of *The Grapes of Wrath* in the *New York Times* of January 25, 1940, Frank Nugent said, among other things:

> In the vast library where the celluloid literature of the screen is stored there is one small, uncrowded shelf devoted to the cinema's masterworks, to those films which by dignity of theme and excellence of treatment seem to be of enduring artistry and seem to be recalled not merely at the end of their particular year but whenever great motion pictures are mentioned. To that shelf of screen classics Twentieth Century–Fox yesterday added its version of John Steinbeck's "The Grapes of Wrath." . . . Does the picture follow the novel, how closely and how well? The answer is that it has followed the book; has followed it closely, but not with blind, undiscriminating literalness; has followed it so well that no one who has read and admired it should complain of the manner of its screen telling. . . . We could go on with this talk of players, but it would become repetitious because there are too many of them, and too many are perfect in their parts. What we've been trying to say is that "The Grapes of Wrath" is just about as good as any picture has a right to be; if it were any better, we just wouldn't believe our eyes.

: : :

Considering all our problems in Chicago, we left there with fine footage, not only because of the outgoing, pregnant, poor women—clients of the center—but because of the elegant photography Crosby had achieved—not only the indoor scenes, under great difficulty, but also the travel shots of the unbelievable wooden slum houses.

We had only a few weeks of time left organizing our Hollywood production sequences when our whole organization was, for all intents and purposes, closed down. Under a reorganization bill, the U.S. Film Service had been transferred from the National Emergency Council to the Department of Education. The commissioner of that outfit was Dr. John S. Studebaker. He was from Iowa, and with that dry, nasal accent he could talk in a monotone for an uninterrupted hour without expressing a single understandable thought.

The Federal Security Agency had also been established by the Reorganization Act of 1939, and the Department of Education had been placed under that agency. One Paul V. McNutt, a former governor of Indiana and a former commander of the American Legion, had been appointed head of the Federal Security Agency. I mentioned that gentleman because there had been a switch made in the Reorganization Act at the last moment, and we had been taken away from the White House, to whom we were responsible under the terms of the original draft of the Reorganization Act, just as were the Archives, the Tennessee Valley Authority, and other independent government agencies.

We had not only been shifted away from the White House, but we had also been left penniless.

Tom Corcoran or James Rowe must have told the president of the trouble that went on the minute I was transferred over to the Office of Education, as President Roosevelt himself wrote a letter to Paul McNutt on November 25, 1939:

> I have been informed that there exists a need for clarification of a portion of my letter which reads ". . . administered in the Office of Education under the direction and supervision of the Administrator of the Federal Security Administration." I feel that the unique needs of a Federal film service . . . require that both authority and responsibility for the prosecution of this program be centralized as much as possible.
>
> I direct, therefore, that the Director of the Film Service assume complete executive and administrative responsibility, under your direction and supervision, for the successful carrying out of the entire program of the United States Film Service.

The president reiterated his desire that all films under way be completed and said that they were not to be construed as being in competition with the commercial product but bore the same relation to Hollywood films as government-printed pamphlets and reports did to commercial books and magazines.

After the completion and the successful opening and distribution of *The Fight for Life* I knew that not only because of the enmity of the Office of Education but also because of the war in Europe I was on my way out of government service. I gave an interview to William O. Player, Jr., of the *New York Post* on May 23, 1940. He wrote a splendid article, a key part being the following:

> The Office of Education not only hadn't produced a single picture or put up one penny toward producing one, but it had for years had many pleasant connections with the Will Hays office in Hollywood and with Hollywood corporations. And the Hays offices [*sic*] from the beginning had been opposed to my making pictures—particularly pictures that were good enough to get on commercial screens.

Years later I found out we had been really stabbed in the back in a number of places and by a number of people while we were busy with four motion picture productions: *Ecce Homo*; *The Fight for Life*; *The Land*, which was being done by Robert Flaherty for the Agriculture Department at their request; and *Power and the Land*, which was being made by Joris Ivens for the Rural Electrification Administration. We simply did not have enough administrative people in high places to watch out for the paperwork from the various agencies supposedly in charge of putting up the money for our work. The result was not only did we not have enough funds for the moment, but beginning at the end of the governmental fiscal year, which was June 30 in those days, we didn't have enough money of *any kind* for the coming year.

Unbeknownst to me, John had received letters from Mrs. Roosevelt about his books and his writings about the migrants, so he casually told me that he had wired her for help when we were told we were penniless. At the time I did not know he already had been publicly praised by Mrs. Roosevelt. Herewith is a copy John gave me of a note to Mrs. Roosevelt from the director of the budget:

> I am returning a telegram of John Steinbeck with reference to the continuation of the work now being performed by the United States Film Service.
>
> I have been advised by officials of the National Emergency Council that arrangements have been made with the Works Progress Administration to provide the necessary funds for the com-

pletion of the picture now in course of production. Question of providing funds for any future productions has not been determined at this time.

(Signed) Harold D. Smith
Director

John also wired the governor of California, Mr. Culbert L. Olson:

San Francisco, California
June 14, 1939

John Steinbeck
Garden of Allah Apts.
Sunset Blvd.
Hollywood, California
Complying with your telegram received today I have telegraphed the president calling his attention to emergency and making request you suggest.

Culbert L. Olson
Governor of California

I don't think he told me about that at the time. I'm sure his pleas were forwarded to President Roosevelt. I'm sure also were the pleas of Paul de Kruif and Surgeon General Tom Parran. Some years later, when we both were out of military service, James Rowe, who had been general counsel of the National Emergency Council, told me that President Roosevelt himself had called Secretary of the Treasury Henry Morgenthau and had told him he wished my appropriation to be the first money to be set aside out of the new budget for 1939–40. Here is the directive the president sent Dr. John Studebaker, commissioner of education, on July 1, 1939:

I have been informed that the Administrator of the Federal Works Administration and the Secretary of Agriculture feel that the completion and distribution by the Film Service of the two motion pictures related to the work relief program which it now has in production are necessary to help effectuate their programs in dealing with the problem of unemployment. I direct, therefore, that the program of production and distribution of these pictures be continued. For this project I am approving an expenditure of $168,000 (Federal Works Agency: WPA, $91,800; Federal

Emergency Administrator of Public Works, $60,000 and Department of Agriculture: Farm Security Administration, $16,700). This project shall be subject to the restrictions and limitations of the Acts from which the funds are derived.

I sent John a telegram October 17, 1939, from my offices in New York City:

> 347 Madison Avenue
> New York, N.Y.
> October 17, 1939

John Steinbeck
Los Gatos, California

Still not on the payroll and in a fancy mess of bureaucracy but the head man as usual wants something done about it which is enough for me. Fine being with you both here. Glad you went away.

> Pare

As I noted earlier, the last shooting of *The Fight for Life* was on the day England declared war on Germany, September 2. I went full-out with my composer, Louis Gruenberg, after that time, but as late as the middle of October our checks had not come through, or at least mine had not come through. Nevertheless, all hands worked industriously once they heard about the president's actions on our behalf.

Dudley Digges and Myron McCormick both had returned to New York, and I needed them to record—in Myron's case, the night walk, and in Dudley's case, the soliloquy over the blood-testing sequence. Gruenberg was content to work with me in New York, as he had a brother and many acquaintances living in the city. The final score was recorded back in Hollywood at the Sam Goldwyn studios by Gordon Sawyer and his partner Lanning just before the Christmas holidays.

Whether John and Carol had domestic problems at this time or not, she did not go with John when he moved over to the Aloha Apartments. Shortly after he went there I was told that he was in severe pain and could hardly walk. Dr. Benaron had come out at my request, as I have noted earlier, so I asked him to look at John for me. He went over to the Aloha and came back saying that John was in intractable pain and that when he saw him, he was on the floor biting a chair leg in agony. I believe Benaron prescribed some temporary pain-relieving nostrum. He himself, being an obstetrician, didn't feel inclined to diagnose John's problem and said we should get hold of a neurologist.

I thought of calling the few men I knew in Hollywood, but I held back because I knew enough anecdotes about corrupt and blackmailing doctors who preyed on their Hollywood clients either by practicing bum medicine or by leaking out their patient's problems to the gossip columnists. John had enough active enemies and enough public fame that I didn't trust any doctor we might find without having secure references. I finally hit upon the idea of calling Dr. Max Peet.

Prior to our starting work on *The Fight for Life*, Paul de Kruif had asked me to show *The Plow That Broke the Plains* and *The River* to a small group in Chicago. They included Dr. Joseph B. De Lee, founder of the Maternity Center, and Dr. Henry Benaron and Dr. Beatrice Tucker, codirectors of the center, and Paul's good friend Dr. Max Peet, professor of neurosurgery at the University of Michigan Medical School. Dr. Peet became a good friend of mine indeed, but that was later on. After the show in Chicago, Dr. De Lee said two things to me: "I think saving the land is more important than saving people's lives," and "Young man, I am going to furnish your brain."

I can say for the fierce old martinet that after one short visit to the center, he never interfered with anything I was doing and trusted the reports and judgments of his young codirectors, Benaron and Tucker, completely.

After the showing, Dr. Peet had only one statement: "I feel as though I've been in a cathedral." You can't help liking a man who says things like that.

Peet was big but not burly, and he often carried a matchbox in each coat pocket in which he had pieces of suture, and he would, while walking or even talking, practice tying knots in the matchboxes. He performed an operation for which he was famous which consisted of boring a peephole into the skull and cutting a nerve or some nerves which carried the terrible pain of facial neuritis. He later on asked me if I would photograph his operation, and he scared the daylights out of me. I just couldn't see myself responsible for forcing a camera around in a man's brain. He argued that we wouldn't need lights, as the cells of the brain would reflect light enough.

Dr. Peet was kind of stagestruck, which explained his interest in movies and literature and the theater. He urged me more than once to tell him something about the lives of some of the more prominent stars of the day, which I didn't do. I preferred telling him something of the rascality of the managers of the industry.

I called his office in Michigan in order to have him give a reference to a local trustworthy neurologist. He was off in Canada, big game fishing and staying in some remote lodge. I had him tracked down finally, and he was pretty surly when he finally got to the phone. He did, however, recommend a neurologist who was also a personal friend, once I had explained my perturbations. Fortunately the doctor was in, and fortunately he was aware of my concern over publicity, so there was never a word printed to my knowledge of John's painful illness and of his medical advisor.

One sundown when I went over after work to the Aloha to see how John was doing, some of his old friends, including Max Wagner, came in bearing a Mexican dinner, all cooked and ready to heat up, and bringing with them also a rather dumpy-looking girl whom they characterized as being a dancer.

Enter Gwyn.

My main worry about John's associaton with Gwyn was that he would take her to Mexico or to New York City or somewhere out of state and that some tough ambulance-chaser might persuade Carol to sue John for everything he owned, down to his underwear. I asked Nunnally Johnson to help me out with John, and the three of us met at Johnson's home one afternoon, where we kindly told John he was getting more famous by the moment and that meant he would certainly be more vulnerable. I begged John to go home and think a while. By home I suggested Cannery Row or his friend Ed's, or he could come to New York and enjoy whatever company in the literary world he chose.

He was noncommittal, yet I think he was aware that we weren't worried about his morality but, more, we were concerned he would get into deep legal and financial problems.

Before I took off for New York City to attend to the problems of the other movies then being made for the Film Service, my governmental financial problems, and the score being done by my gifted composer, Louis Gruenberg, it happened that a member of my staff for whom I had reserved a plane ticket had an emergency call and had to go on ahead of me. I still had his reservation, and I begged John to come with me. He went as far as to say he would meet me in the bar at the airport and give me his decision. He met me there, all right, and he was accompanied by his mother-in-law to be and her young boyfriend, who looked younger than John.

She was a sharp-faced lady dressed in pink satin slacks. She and the boyfriend both worked in one of the new national defense aircraft factories. I don't know what John wished me to say in such company, but he did look sheepish and said that he had decided he'd better stay in Hollywood for the time being. Years after Gwyn divorced John, or vice-versa (I don't know which), one of the editors of Viking Press said that John had walked into the office recently and belligerently had said that he was probably their best-selling author and his books had been translated and sold all over the world, yet he wasn't getting any money back. One of the editors looked up and said to John:

"You forget John—those wives, those wives!"

So I gather the ladies did find tough lawyers.

∶　∶　∶

I have no records of the dates, but I keep remembering John's presence in New York as well as in California as I proceeded to finish *The Fight for Life*.

Louis Gruenberg was a pleasure to work with as the composer. He was totally dedicated to the subject matter. He had married late in life a titled Czech woman, and they had a little girl child. I didn't meet the lady. All during our relationship Louis was extremely concerned about not only some of his relatives in Austria but also her relatives and her property in Czechoslovakia.

There was nothing I could do to help him save to try to get his attention concentrated on our work. While he waited for me to get a final cut of the film, he worked on the score in New York City. We had agreed upon sequences and the nature of the music, so somewhere in October or November he arranged to come to Sneden's Landing and play the entire score on the good Steinway piano that was in the living room of my rented house, which was known as Captain John's House.

Paul de Kruif and his wife, Rhea; John; and my good editor at *McCall's*, Otis Wiese, were the guests. The score was beautiful. It ran fifty-five minutes (which made it the longest musical score ever written for a nonmusical movie). At the conclusion, Gruenberg slammed his hand down on the piano, making a loud, dissonant tone, and said: "God damn, I've written a symphony!"

He didn't add, "at government wages," but he never complained about the low amount of money he was getting. On the contrary, he said that it was a delight not to have to write "Bury me not on the lone prairie" in five keys, which he had had to do for John Ford with *Stagecoach*.

He also once told me that he had written the opera *Emperor Jones* for the Metropolitan Opera Company for a flat fee—no royalties—of five hundred dollars. Louis had been the last pupil of Richard Strauss before he emigrated to America, and the first composition he wrote in America was called "Daniel Jazz."

Steinbeck's reaction was extraordinary. He looked up at Paul de Kruif and said, "People are no damn good and I'm never going to write about them again. I'm going to write about bugs." Later on he got to talking to Paul about what later became *The Sea of Cortez*.

Sometime in this period, my superior, Lowell Mellett, asked me casually when I expected to have the finished movie, now that I had funds to complete it. I said New Year's Day, 1940, and he replied: "I'll see if I can make arrangements for you to show it to the president New Year's Eve." And he did.

I remember the week before Christmas vividly. There were four of us in the cutting room, and we worked long after midnight every night. About one or two in the morning I'd send out for swiss cheese sandwiches and coffee, and we'd turn up the radio and do a little shuffle in the cutting room. The swing shift had already started for the new defense factories, and the radio broadcast some of the best jazz I ever heard during those single-digit hours.

I spent Christmas Eve completely alone except for one waiter and the cook at Dave Chasen's restaurant. Lloyd Nosler, my fine editor, had a drink with me before going off to *his* Christmas party, saying that we had paid our negative cutters for 112 hours of work that week.

We were so concerned about getting to the White House in good order that I had a second master print made, and we shipped it on a different airplane than the one I traveled on with the original master.

Carol reported to John that the president didn't like *The Fight for Life*. That is an error. It was *Mrs.* Roosevelt who helped me get in trouble with one group of doctors before I could get out of Washington and start previewing in New York City.

I didn't keep the clipping of her column, "My Day," but it started off talking about the showing at the White House and misnaming the picture *"The Struggle for Life"* and then remarking that it wasn't a good idea to show it, as it would frighten any young woman having a child, or some such words.

What happened at the White House is as follows: I was worn to the bone. Besides that, I always got buck fever whenever I stepped on the great seal of the United States of America built into the entrance of the White House. (Considering who has walked on it in recent years, they should cover it with a floor mat.)

Mrs. Roosevelt sat me next to Joe Alsop, who was sitting next to Secretary of the Treasury Morgenthau. Joe Alsop at that time was a newspaper columnist for the *New York Herald Tribune*. Mrs. Roosevelt herself had chosen the entertainment for the evening with no regard to the fact that I was showing a feature motion picture.

Before we were all seated, those of us who had not had dinner with the president before watched the president come through the door and wheel his way up to the front of the room in his wheelchair. Behind came two Episcopalian bishops dressed in velvet knee breeches, both of them haranguing the president's mother, Mrs. James Roosevelt, about what she was going to do with her home in Hyde Park in her will. They were smoking long cigars that would have done credit to very prosperous movie producers.

The president spied me and interrupted the bishops' interrogation long enough to look at me and introduce me, saying: "He's my shooter. He photographs America to show what it's like to our people." The bishops looked annoyed but broke off their interrogation and joined the crowd.

The first thing that took place to start off New Year's Eve was a series of newsreels. The president always wanted to see newsreels when he had a movie night. These were pretty gory. I remember only the main one, which was a shot of a series of bodies of Chinese dead laid out artistically on the steps of some important building in Shanghai. They had been killed by shelling from the Japanese navy. Unlike other times, the president did not say a word of any kind during this whole prologue to my showing.

Next came a very untalented middle-aged lady, who did a lengthy pantomime that consisted of her showing a man being seized, beaten, and put in a concentration camp. At the conclusion of the performance she fell on her knees in front of the president and put her hands up in supplication, pleading that he get her loved one out of the concentration camp.

By now time was running out, and I told Mrs. Roosevelt that there might not be time enough to show my movie because it might go past midnight. (I didn't say it, but meant if she had any other acts to present.) She assured me there was time and then whispered that she'd have to leave and go attend Franklin Jr. and his new bride Ethel du Pont, as they both were being seen by the president's doctor, Admiral McIntyre, because they had hit or had been hit by a truck on their drive back from Charlottesville, where Franklin, Jr., was attending law school.

Just before midnight there was some commotion out in the hall and there was a crash. Son John Roosevelt, in white tie, had attended a party of his own and had fallen down the stairs, breaking the flask he was carrying in his hip pocket, so Dr. McIntyre had to sew up John's rear.

Finally, *The Fight for Life.*

As it started, Joe Alsop turned to Secretary Morgenthau and said, "This is about socialized medicine so why don't we go someplace and talk," whereupon the two of them got up, Morgenthau obediently following Alsop out, seeking some White House nook where the secretary of the treasury could be educated by Mr. Joseph Alsop.

The movie ended just a few minutes before midnight. Quickly a servant brought a little banged-up portable radio and put it on the president's desk. The president wheeled himself to his desk. Another servant brought in a beautiful, large punch bowl. We were all offered and took cups, and the president regarded his watch and turned on the little radio. Meantime he took a call, which was one he had arranged to his son James, who was in Hollywood. He wished James a happy new year and then took his cup of punch and said, "And this is my annual toast."

I saw him looking around trying to catch somebody's eye. Some of his grandchildren had come downstairs in their nightclothes. There was a shaking of hands, pounding of backs, and kissing on cheeks, and I went to Mrs. Roosevelt and said that I wished to go, as it was a family party and I didn't want to intrude. She countered by saying that the president wanted to speak with me and would I please stand in line and speak with him.

The president finally raised his punch cup and looked me square in the eye and said again, "This is my annual toast: to the people of the United States!"

Before this I noticed that the president's mother was sitting catty-cornered in the president's study observing the goings-on, so I went over to her first and wished her a happy new year. She looked up at me frostily and said, "It's an interesting movie but I don't think it should be shown in mixed company." For a while I felt as though I had shown a pornographic movie of *Up in Mabel's Room* or some such epic, and I was indeed downhearted.

When the president shook my hand, he smiled, as I'm sure he saw the expression on my face after I spoke with his mother, and he said in a kind, fatherly voice, "That's a fine movie and I hope it does a lot of *good*," which he announced in a positive tone.

He then said, "When are you going to get *Ecce Homo* done?" Taken aback, I thought and said, "Probably by May 1."

The president said formally, "I'd like to have it by then so I can call a special session of the whole Congress and show it to them before I present the river valley proposal to them."

I had a sinking feeling that there was no way this could be accomplished. He had done the same thing on *The River* when I showed it to him in Hyde Park and he said that he wanted to show *The River* to a joint session of Congress. But I was so shaken that I never called attention to his idea again.

Carol was wrong. I didn't see her after that showing. It was not that the president was against the movie; it was more that the times and a few people who were deeply jealous of Dr. Joseph de Lee were against the film. I found that out as I went along peddling my work.

I wrote John a resume May 15, 1940, which did not go into any details but does represent a record of my activities and of my feelings at that time that I was through with government service.

Mr. Roosevelt had not yet declared for his third term when I wrote this letter to John, nor had the Germans started to burn down England with their air raids, although they were to start that action in only two weeks from the time I wrote John. France was to fall in a matter of three or four weeks. No time indeed to concern oneself with maternal and infant welfare.

Once I got over my gloom, which was justified by the sad yet tense atmosphere emanating from the president's New Year's Eve gathering, I decided to get *The Fight for Life* distributed come hell or high water, and I spent days and nights attending to the other productions for which I was responsible: *The Land*, being done by Robert Flaherty, and *Power and the Land*, being done by Joris Ivens. In each case, rather than taking time out from exhibiting *The Fight for Life* and battling the Department of Education for funds for movies which had been requested by other departments, I turned the production of both *The Land* and *Power and the Land* over to the Rural Electrification Administration and the Department of Agriculture, which had requested them in the first place.

I was perfectly willing to have my technical crew, led by Lloyd Nosler, probably one of the most experienced film editors in the business, work on the films done under the direction of the directors, but neither Ivens nor Flaherty would accept anybody but Helen van Dongen, probably the most banal and redundant film editor ever to handle motion pictures, particularly important and sometimes beautiful films.

John wrote me an interesting letter on February 26, 1940, while I was galloping off in all directions. I didn't get to answer it until two months later. My letter follows John's.

Los Gatos, California
February 26, 1940

Mr. Pare Lorentz
U.S. Film Service
341 Madison Avenue
New York, N.Y.

Dear Pare:

I don't know whether you are still in Florida or not. Pat Covici writes that it is cold and miserable in New York. Well it has rained for seven days here and looks as though it were going on one of those 21 day bursts. We're stir crazy.

Our permits have not come through to go to Mexico. Maybe they never will. I don't know. Paul undoubtedly told you of the royal kick in the pants we got from the administration. I guess I shot my wad on that thing of yours. I know I could only do it once. So maybe we're going and maybe not. The tenth of March is the latest we can start and still make the tides. We have a boat ready to charter, equipment, everything except permission to go. Maybe Mr. Sumner Welles kicked us so thoroughly in Mexico that we can't get permission. They have a bad political situation there this year. I'm getting a little sour on governments.

About your strong beef about pictures from my mss. You know perfectly well that if you were making private pictures, you could have any of them. That should be proven by the fact that you still hold "In Dubious Battle." But you aren't making them. In the matter of "The Red Pony," I made a bluff. If even a bad picture made of one of my mss. could turn over a large chunk of money to hospitals, I'd be willing. But the bluff wasn't called and that was that. So don't you start a bluff. When you are ready to make private films, I'll go along to the limit with you. But I'm beginning to believe that the Hayes office and a vacillating administration don't offer much choice. There is expediency in both cases, the one mercenary and the other political. I don't understand either part of it and so I'm not going to play with it. *I discovered in my little time with you that picture making is too complicated for my narrow gauge mind and so I'll have nothing active to do with it from now on.* I'm too often out of my depth.

I hope you are calmed down now and your temperature back to normal. Jesus! How it is raining. No envelopes in the house. Don't know where I'll send this. I'll see you some time. If we go south I'll see you in six months and if we don't, I'll see you sooner.

John

May 15, 1940

Mr. John Steinbeck
Los Gatos, California

Dear John:

I am several months late in writing this letter but that is about the normal period of what we call government lag.

I understand you are in Mexico now but I hope this letter either will be forwarded to you or that you will get it when you return.

After I came back from Florida the last of February, I discovered we had no theatre in which to open THE FIGHT FOR LIFE and I knew that we were to be given the works by some members of Congress so, by all of us working days and night, we were able to launch a very successful if small and quiet opening.

We immediately got into a running fight with the New York Medical Society and two or three disgruntled doctors, and as Dr. Parran and most of the government men who were supposed to be interested in public health refused to enter into the controversy, we had to bail ourselves out. We had weeks of digging into research and writing letters to the New York Times and in general running a public health agency and we were able to win completely but it was a nerve wracking and unnecessary experience.

We put on a series of previews for the Rockefeller Institute and for medical groups in Baltimore and Dayton and Chicago, and in general got about six weeks of showings under our belts before we attempted to hit the Hollywood distributors. We got an amazing response from theatre owners based on the reviews and for the first time proved that we didn't need a major studio in order to guarantee a release.

Meantime, we were finally sabotaged completely by Dr. John Studebaker and Paul V. McNutt in that they put our appropriations before Congress in a lackadaisical and illegal manner so besides trying to deal with theatre owners with my left hand, I spent six solid weeks going to Washington, making up budgets, and working with lawyers and trying to rescue the United States Film Service. Actually, what happened to us was that neither Lowell Mellett, nor Harold Ickes, nor Tom Corcoran, nor any of the men close to the President had any time to devote to our work because they were interested in the war, so that we were voted down a few weeks ago by the Senate in our request for appropriations because no one in Washington brought any pressure to bear for us.

We are opening up our contracts today and will have either the best of the independents or probably Columbia Pictures take over the movie. We will open in Washington and Chicago and Hollywood as soon after we award the contract as possible and then the staff has to look for jobs, including myself.

I am trying to get King's agent to set up an independent corporation with an independent release so that I could take the same crew we have and make one picture at least on an independent basis. I am devoting the month of June to this work and will be two weeks on the coast and two weeks in New York, but if it doesn't come off, I will probably write a book about what we did and what we tried to do these past five years and what we saw of the country while we were doing it.

The picture received higher praise than we could have hoped for but it has been an unpleasant winter because we have lacked any support out of Washington and it has made us feel as though we were working in a vacuum.

It has been a generally dispiriting time, except for the fact that the picture continues to run and make friends and influence people.

I am very curious naturally to know what you are doing and hope it is a story of the Irishmen down at the end of Mexico.

We will have our offices in the Goldwyn Studios up until the end of June, and at 347 Madison Avenue also until the end of June, and I will be part time here and part time in the West, hoping to nail down "The Fight for Life" for good, and to liquidate this office and get my people work and to have some sort of hope of working independent of Hollywood myself.

Let me hear from you if you have time and if we go to war this unit probably will try to get in Washington before Cecil de Mille does.

Yours,
Pare

: : :

In his letter to me of February 26, a few pages back, I underlined John's statement about his feelings about his moviemaking because Professor DeMott described John's experience with Herb Kline in Mexico as being a clash of wills as well as a class of skills.

I know that Lloyd Nosler offered to help John but did not try to impose himself on the project for *The Forgotten Village*. He would have saved John a great deal of physical effort and personal exasperation if he had had a man of Nosler's experience to do all the menial jobs of splicing, rewinding, categorizing out-takes, and so on.

The next time I saw John was again in Sneden's Landing. My time

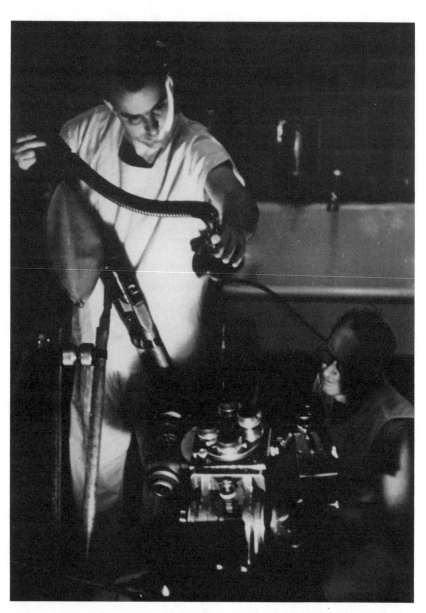

Pare Lorentz (left) and Floyd Crosby, chief cameraman, examining hand tests of a scene from The Fight for Life.

"They brought them into all our great cities from the hills and fields to build their machines and roll their steel . . . and left them in these shacks." From The Fight for Life.

Myron McCormick as Dr. O'Donnell, an intern, and Dudley Digges as the head doctor.
From The Fight for Life.

there was getting to be short. One morning John and my wife, Sally, disappeared for a while, and upon their return I questioned him. I was told that John had been looking for a house to rent. Later that afternoon John went trotting alongside me as we walked. He frisked about like a schoolboy preparing to attend his first prom. That evening the reason for his mysterious behavior appeared in the person of Gwyn, whom he had brought with him to Sneden's Landing.

It was only this year that I found out which house he had rented. It was called "The House in the Woods," and it was where I lived as a young bachelor and where I had written the book I wrote with Morris L. Ernst, *Censored: The Private Life of the Movies.*

Save for that walk through the park in 1943 and our chance meeting on the threshold of the 21 Club, I never saw John again. We did correspond sporadically and kept track of each other's work up until he arrived with Gwyn in Sneden's Landing prior to his divorce and his wedding.

I'm sorry I didn't go over to the Bedford and have that cup of coffee. It would have turned into a long night.

don't remember who in the U.S. government ordered me to go to Chicago to exhibit *The Fight for Life* to Morris Fishbein, editor of the *Journal of the American Medical Association*; Dr. De Lee; and the staff of the Chicago Maternity Center and members of the Chicago Medical Society, but when I heard that I was going to have to go alone, I absolutely refused to be a clay pigeon for all concerned.

Paul de Kruif was in Pompano Beach, Florida. I finally located him by sending a local policeman to look for him and getting him to a telephone booth. I told him he would have to send some friendly and important escort for me, preferably a medical doctor. Paul told me to wait where I was. In a few minutes he called me back and said Dr. Max Peet would come down from medical school to hold my hand while we had the showing.

Fishbein was hardly inclined to like anything presented by the U.S. government, as he had been sued by the Justice Department for running a union in restraint of trade (the American Medical Association). Besides that, he was a very reactionary and vain man.

The showing was in the Breasted Museum at the University of Chicago, which, besides having a small theater and projection booth, housed King Tut's mummy. The whole room was gloomy and reflected the gloomy artifacts on exhibit.

As soon as we turned on the film, Dr. Fishbein started talking. One of the good doctors asked him to be quiet finally, and we were able to finish the film without his observations. However, the minute the movie was over, he said: "I want to stop that film and look at it when it's not running."

Dr. De Lee hopped on him immediately, bless his soul, and said: "Morris, a movie wasn't made to be shown stopped."

There were some other minor arguments until suddenly Fishbein spied Dr. Max Peet, who outranked everybody there, and said: "Dr. Peet, what do *you* think of the movie?"

I was melancholy and concerned but should not have been. Dr. Peet looked up and said: "It has one fault. It is too short."

That did it. All the good people from the Maternity Center were really impressed and pleased and had no complaints of any kind to offer.

After we left the projection room, Dr. Peet turned to me and said: "How did you get a camera on that woman having a hemorrhage?"

I replied by saying that Dr. Benaron had told me that such patients turned white and had great blobs of sweat on their faces. We did this with Dorothy Adams, making her up in off-white to match the off-white bedclothes to cut down on the glare. Dr. Benaron also added that they yawned a great deal, and I had to refrain from laughing, as that would have been a great life-and-death scene—six or seven big yawns.

Dr. Peet shook his head and said: "No, what I'm talking about is that look she has. I've seen it too often." That was one of several great compliments I had about making that movie.

I then explained to Dr. Peet that I had been troubled from the beginning as to how to direct a scene in which the patient looks at the doctor and says, "You won't let me die, will you doctor?" In one way it was a cornball sentence to try to dramatize. I hit upon the solution by telling Dorothy that the only way I could see to do that scene correctly was to make it a love scene. I cleared the set except for the necessary technicians and got a stool which I put right under the cameras so that Dorothy would look right at me. I spoke softly to her and said: "I may be the last man you ever see on this earth."

She was tired enough from carrying around the heavy weight which I had her strap on so that she would have what is called a pregnant strut in her big scene before her last hemorrhage scene.

That is the look that Dr. Peet had seen on many of his patients' faces.

: : :

I returned to New York still downhearted because no one had suggested that they might help me get distribution among the good people who liked the film in Chicago. What I did then was to turn to my friends and acquaintances.

One was Dr. Frank McGowan, a neurosurgeon. He solicited the directors of the New York Academy of Medicine, with the result that they issued an engraved invitation to all their members to attend a viewing of the film at one of the projection rooms at what was then Radio City Music Hall.

Among the directors of the academy was Dr. James Alexander Miller. His daughter and son-in-law—Peggy and Dan Lindley—were very close friends of mine, and he was enthusiastic about the showing. In fact, Dr. Miller introduced me to the members before the viewing of the film, saying, "I don't know anything about his movie. All I know is he drinks my whiskey with my son-in-law and daughter."

After the showing, Dr. Miller again chaired the event and asked for remarks. A Dr. Woodruff spoke first, saying that he had interned at the Chicago Maternity Center as a young medical student and the movie was a fine portrait of the center and its work. Finally, somebody asked Dr. Miller what *he* thought of it. He started, "I have one criticism. . . ." There I went again, but what he said was, "there are no bum doctors in the film."

Finally, Paul de Kruif arranged for me to go to Dayton, Ohio, and to talk with Dr. Walt Simpson, chief pathologist at the Miami Valley Hospital. He also was a director of Charles Franklin "Boss" Kettering's medical foundation.

After talking to Simpson, I met with Kettering, who said he would be willing to put up five million dollars for the production of medical motion pictures if de Kruif and Walt chose the topic and I made the films. It's the only time I was ever offered five million dollars to make movies my way, but I knew the war was coming and that I would be in it. But they certainly were a fine group of men.

Peggy Lindley had heard on the radio somewhere that the word had gone out, because of Mrs. Roosevelt's column "My Day," that women would be frightened after seeing this film, so Peggy rounded up a half-dozen very pretty, quite rich socialites who were very pregnant. They were all members of a New York Maternity Society and devoted some time and money to the gynecologist who was the chairman of their little society. They were very complimentary about the film, but they raised hell with the doctor on the grounds that the women being attended by the doctors at the Chicago Maternity Center in the slums of the city were getting better prenatal, delivery, and postnatal care than their doctor was giving them. It turned out that the doctor was exceedingly jealous of Dr. De Lee to begin with, so he got the New York County Medical Society to write a letter to the *New York Times* denouncing my movie.

The *Times* called me and asked if I had anything to say about the letter. I said, "Considerable and most of it profane," and I ended up calling the New York County Medical Society a bunch of quacks.

When this letter appeared in the *New York Sunday Times*, Dr. Miller called me immediately and scolded me heartily, saying, "You must never call doctors quacks, even if they are."

Someone told me about the Belmont Theater, and I made arrangements to open there. I had the chance for once in my life to seat several hundred people exactly where I wanted them, based on their ability and their knowledge of film and their general contribution to society. I turned the gallery over completely to my club, the Players, as at least two members of the cast, besides myself, were members. The notices, some of which I include here, were magnificent, and we played in the Belmont for many weeks, during which time Columbia Pictures took over the film for distribution.

One final anecdote: I dealt with the sales manager of Columbia, who was a polite fellow and, as I remember, a champion senior tennis player. When we got down to the final negotiations, Abe turned to me and said, "There's one thing. I want you to take that Communist scene out of the picture."

I asked him politely what in the hell scene was "Communist" in my film. Finally, after he tried to remember, he said, "That big grey cat in the alley."

When we were doing the final cutting, I had remembered that that was one of the short shots I had made to allow a break in any scene where birth was imminent. I remembered that old grey, fierce alley cat, so I said that we would use that short scene for the cut away. We had started looking and went through every can of out-takes in the cutting room. It was getting towards morning, and, so help me, it was the very last piece of film in the very last can of film.

I told Abe that it was my favorite scene in the film and I would not take it out.

One other anecdote: I had a diligent production helper, named Oliver Griswold, from the Washington office. He was very dapper, with a neat mustache, and in the winter he wore an overcoat with an astrakhan collar.

I needed a few pregnant women in Los Angeles to be in a reception room scene, so I sent Ollie out to recruit them. He was at Griffith Park in front of the fountain when he spied a good-looking lady who was very pregnant, and he approached her saying, "I have a proposition for you." With that, she pushed him right into the fountain.

Will Geer knew I was searching for folk singers for my movie *Ecce Homo*. He brought me Woody Guthrie, who was singing on a little one-lung radio station and writing a column in the Communist publication *People's World*. I had him sit with an extra on the steps outside a slum door on the Columbia Pictures set and had him look like he was playing the guitar while I actually had two Mexicans playing my theme song for the film, "The Sick Rose Bush." I had a policeman go by saying, "What's going on in there?"

The extra replies, "Oh, just a woman having a baby."

THE

FIGHT

FOR

LIFE

(*A United States Film Service Production*)

Screenplay by Pare Lorentz

Adapted from the Maternal Welfare Chapters of
   The Fight for Life by Paul de Kruif

Produced and Directed by Pare Lorentz

Musical Score by Louis Gruenberg

Orchestra Conducted by Alexander Smallens

The Cast
O'Donnell, An Intern: Myron McCormick
Dr. Ballou: Storrs Haynes
Dr. Hanson: Will Geer
Head Doctor, at the City Hospital: Dudley Digges
Young Woman: Dorothy Adams
Grandmother: Dorothy Urban
Receptionist: Effie Anderson
and Doctors, Students, Nurses, Women of the City

Only those familiar with the grave national problem of infant and maternal mortality know the heroic fight which is being waged on a little-known front against needless death.

The Fight for Life is a motion picture dramatization, for the public, of the effort to bring the skills of modern science to the poor women of a great city. The film is based on the book of the same name written by Paul de Kruif, author of *Microbe Hunters, Hunger Fighters, Men Against Death*, and other works.

Here in 68 minutes is an elemental drama of life and death—a saga of medical science and its work in the slums of a great city—the problem society faces and what can be done about it.

The Fight for Life begins with death and ends with life.

In a great hospital, a woman is having a baby. Young Dr. O'Donnell and his assistants fight desperately to save her life as complications develop. But as they win their fight to bring one life into the world they lose their battle to save the mother's life.

Bewildered, O'Donnell seeks advice from the Head Doctor at the County Hospital, who advises him to go to the Maternity Center. There, two doctors, Ballou and Hanson, are applying the techniques of modern science to the care of tenement mothers. O'Donnell goes to the Center, where, as the young Intern, he learns these techniques, assists with deliveries in the slum homes, and becomes expert in bringing life into the world under adverse and dangerous conditions.

Several representative cases of maternity treatment are depicted. But O'Donnell is to have the final proof of his ability to join these men against death in a case for which he alone is responsible. Although he delivers the infant safely, the mother develops a hemorrhage, and Dr. O'Donnell and his assistants are shown battling to save the mother's life. He sends to the "blood bank" for blood for transfusion and to the Center for the two doctors to assist in an emergency operation. The battle won to save this mother's life, O'Donnell's faith in himself is restored as he returns to the Center to continue to heal the sick and, in turn, to teach others.

Over two-thirds of *The Fight for Life* was shot silently, in the Chicago Maternity Centre, Chicago Lying-In, and in tenement homes of expectant mothers, most of whom were relief clients. The housing pictures were shot in the industrial cities of the Midwest. The direct dialogue sequences were shot in Hollywood, the furniture and some of the sets being brought from actual locations so the dialogue, narrative, and silent sequences could be matched. The soliloquies were narrated after the musical score had been written and edited with the final cut of the picture.

PREFACE

Pare Lorentz's Music Instructions for *The Fight for Life*

This memorandum never was intended for publication, but I asked the authors to include it because *The Fight for Life* was so much a musical picture the bare text seems meaningless without at least some mention of the score and how it was created, and because I felt it might help explain the technical construction of the picture.

It is reprinted here exactly as I sent it to Louis Gruenberg; reading it now I find it is not only an awkward bit of writing, but is such a shorthand description of the intent of the whole story I can understand why, when he first read it, Louis went reeling home talking to himself.

What I had done was to direct a picture to unwritten music and then ask a composer to write it, as, in fact, I did with *The Plow That Broke the Plains* and *The River*. Both Virgil Thomson, who wrote the scores for the first two pictures, and Gruenberg worked in the cutting room with us as collaborators and gave a continuity and an emotional content to the work that was simpler, and more powerful in many sequences than any words could have been, and I am eternally grateful to them.

PARE LORENTZ

TITLES. 1½ minutes.

LIFE. From the opening scene in the picture—which is a tilt up to a sign saying "City Hospital" until the end of this sequence, this part of the picture will be rigidly edited to metronome time—it is the one sequence that needs synchronization, and not interpretation of any kind, save through an exact beat.

Every scene was directed to a metronome, and for dramatic effect the music must start exactly with the film—from the moment we see "City Hospital" until the baby is born, the beat of the music must not vary, and there must be no change in instrumentation sufficient enough to be noticeable—the conception in direction was that we would have the mother's heart beat—two beats in one, with the accent on the first one; with the echo exactly 1½ times as fast, and without an accent; factually, a beat of 100 a minute as against the fetal heart beat of 150 a minute.

The picture will not be cut with this precision; but the music should have this precision, inasmuch as the nurses and doctors were directed to move within these tempos.

From the opening scene until the birth of the baby, the approximate time—four minutes.

We have a transition here, which is musically a coda that should not be evident; on the film, the characters relax for about half a minute; we see the doctor strolling towards his patient; we see the intern looking at the child; we see a relaxation.

If the music changed here we would have a curtain; in movies, a fade-out.

On the screen we have no fade-out, no dissolve—no momentary interruption of action, so; even though the mood changes, the vision continues.

Thus, the only change in the music should be a change in time.

For 360 feet we had a time dominated by the mother's heart; the tympani concentrates on this beat.

The minute the child is born, the baby's fluttering heart dominates the beat, so for this transition, except for any passage you may like: a trumpet cry: a crescendo—any device you may wish to use for the birth pain—is merely a cue for a different beat.

Within half a minute the doctor discovers the woman is dying— again the film is directed and cut to a specific time—the heart is pounding to hang on—the dramatic change in the score is that suddenly the mother's heart again takes over—the slower beat surges under the baby's heart beat, and instead of growing weaker, musically, the heart grows in volume, if slowing in tempo—it goes—Bang— BANG—BANG———BANG———and death is the sudden cessation of that pulsing beat—and we have only the baby's counterpoint sound to hold our intern until he walks into the corridor and starts for the street.

DEATH—Approximate time—three minutes.

SUMMARY: The picture opens with a duet of bass and tenor drum.

The bass drum dominates the fugue until birth—this is four minutes—the tenor drum increases in volume for half a minute, and then the bass drum suddenly bangs to life and continues to build in volume like a heavy truck struggling under a load to climb a hill until it suddenly cuts out completely, and the faint tenor drum beat carries on—this is three minutes.

There is a second hand which gives us visually a feeling of beat and time; we will show this clock going around three times during the editing of this part of the picture.

There is the coordination of nurses and doctors, working in exact time.

I do not argue that this sequence must have only two drums—

I do feel that any varied orchestration—any development of theme by strings, woodwinds, and brasses—that any ordinary sonata development would disturb the exact beat this section of the film will have visually. I shall edit it to the sound of two drums, each in double beat.

Musically, this is not the beginning of thematic design in the picture—this is not where we introduce a theme of life and death. This is a prologue; the query, the curtain-raiser. This is not the beginning of the story;—*this is the reason we tell a story.* It should be considered apart from the symphonic pattern of the rest of the picture, yet the heartbeat should be so carefully done that we can reiterate and repeat the beat whenever we approach a pregnant woman.

But I do not start the story for many minutes—therefore the music should not start a story.

The music must always precede the picture; the picture must always precede the words—it is our dramatic procedure; also the eye sees faster than the ear hears.

Thus, the minute our intern walks out of the delivery room, suddenly under the one drum we start almost an echo; a far-off sound; or, in radio terms, we start to sneak music under him.

That beat makes it simple; from those drums we start a gut-bucket, barrel-house, gin mill, Rampart Street, belly-rub, low-down, double-shuffle, boogie-woogie, jug-band, blues—call it what you like, it's the old Bessie Smith, one-handed piano player blues—the blues played by the illiterate gulf-coast negroes who had no left hand—who hit the bass with their left thumbs to make sure, and then hit the rest of the chord off-beat; the method, so-called, of Fats Waller.

It is a slow time, with deliberate off-beat; it is a hot, crowded saloon with ten-cent gin, wanton, weary, bedeviled men and women.

(Since 1915 I have heard such music; in Shreveport; in Camden, Arkansas; in Tampico; in Laredo; in Lubbock;—what I mean is that swing and all such esoteric names annoy me; I heard a jug orchestra in army camp in Camp Knox; the heat, the moon, and the loneliness— that is a part of "swing" music.)

I feel, then, that we start one piano under the intern; that we start another piano as he walks out of the hospital; that the minute he hits the street, we suddenly hit the audience in the face with gin, women, despair, cruelty and life, as crude as it is.

Now, here the words create a symphonic pattern. The words themselves carry the meaning and the tempo;—the film and the music continue, not in monotony, but without variation, until that very savage, unrelieved, 4/4 time creates a frightening city.

If the music attempts to narrate the city; to interpret it, then the music and the picture will overwhelm my dialogue.

My man is all-important—he doesn't know where he is.

Thus—he is a sad man who has dropped into a negro saloon.

He is drinking gin and talking to himself. He doesn't know there is an orchestra in the room—he doesn't know there are wanton women around him; he pays no attention to the whores, the savage, primitive emotions; he is worried over his own soul, and the noise merely gives him a background against which to retire.

SUMMARY: The intern walks out of the hospital and talks to himself; the picture is edited in slow time to two pianos playing blues.

NOTE: I think the pianos should start this walk; I have no objection to any orchestration that might come in here, or in any other sequence; however, I feel strongly that there must not be enough variation to interrupt the mood, and where such unvaried music would be unbearable on the concert stage, here it would be noticeable to such a degree that you would think more of the pictures of the city than you would of my man thinking about death.

There is what I mean by third dimension editing—the words, the tempo of the voice give us variation—not the orchestra.

I repeat here so often because twice before I have had this problem—each time the composer felt he had to vary the orchestration;

each time we had to take one phrase of music and repeat it because repetition was better than development.

Maximum time—four minutes.

THE DOCTOR: The intern walks into an old doctor's office, and the doctor begins where the intern left off.

There is no "won't you sit-down," etc.—the doctor continues his philosophy exactly where the intern left off narrating in the streets.

Here I feel we are closing out our prologue, so we have only a subdued recording of our city music—the city is outside, but the doctor talks about it.

Maximum time—three minutes.

NOTE: The delivery room has taken seven minutes, four minutes for life, three minutes for death. The walk through the city has taken four minutes—the doctor has taken three minutes—

Naturally, I do not ask you to have only two drums for seven minutes, and two pianos for seven minutes.

However, I do not want the score to introduce two themes, to develop and recapitulate theme; rather, we should use the orchestra to amplify and augment the beat, for the first seven minutes; and the blues, in the next seven minutes.

Also, these times are over-length—

If I can hear the beats—and the blues—then I can give you the time exact very quickly.

The night walk, however, is one of the three great music-word-picture sections of the picture.

THE MATERNITY CENTER: This section of the film is broken into four exact parts; we have no dialogue until we see poor women coming into the center; see our intern examining a woman; then for 1½ minutes he is instructed.

We dissolve into the broken-down shoes of our patients, the poor women sitting, waiting to be examined; then we see our intern examining a woman; then another 1½ minutes of teaching.

It is then, a musical reel; ten minutes of a study of faces, and of men working with women, interrupted by teaching episodes each of which is shorter than the silent examination scenes.

As all the words are lyrical in the rest of the picture, this always has been the most difficult part of the movie to write and edit.

I think you must wait until I have smoothed out the scenes which are mostly portrait studies of Polish, Mexican, Italian, Jewish, Swedish women sitting patiently waiting their fate—and cut them along with the teaching scenes, until we get a sense of tempo in it.

I think we should have musical rests—deliberately—every time one of the teachers speaks for a minute and a half, rather than putting down volume on a score. Thus, we can make this a musical reel with interruptions—rather than a dialogue reel in which there is occasional music—a very important difference.

You are much more interested in the women than in the teaching in any case, and, perhaps, with the faces, the smooth cutting, and the silent examinations, we can make such an effective picture of our intern learning, that we can cut down the actual words considerably.

Maximum time—ten minutes—five minutes of music.

THE LECTURE: This is a movie within a movie; a home movie is used by the teachers to show the technique the students should use in the tenements—here we give all the figures of maternal mortality, of accident and avoidable death, and, in effect, explain the factual part of obstetrics, so that the audience knows what our intern is about. This should be definitely a musical rest—unless we have failed to provide music for the pregnant women in the preceding reel. This is my most difficult section. But I see these two reels as going—music, close-ups of women, and our intern—silence—teaching—faces, music, and our intern working with music—then silence, words of teaching—then a final lecture with no music.

Time of lecture—ten minutes.

THE TWO TENEMENT HOUSES: The way the picture will be edited is as follows:

Our intern goes on his first case; they prepare the house, they examine the woman.

Then it is night, and they wait; the woman has a pain and they prepare to deliver her.

Suddenly we show the Bulletin Board—we see the woman has had a successful delivery—and as suddenly we dissolve with the board

Chicago Maternity Center crew attending a patient in tenement housing, Chicago, May 1939. From The Fight for Life.

whirling around showing case after case, to mark the fact that our intern has been going out on cases for weeks—then we show him helping a woman who just has had a baby.

This is one reel—ten minutes, but musically, it breaks down as the beginning, and almost the end of a real symphonic development.

First we have the preparation in the tenement.

It is a poor house. It is in the city. There is a pregnant woman in it. Already we have all the score available to use again—had we written a theme for the city, and one for life, and death.

I feel now we can start—that only the heart-beats are available to us, that the music is as new as the scenes.

Visually, this is what happens: A house is made clean, a woman comfortable—three minutes.

It is night—they are waiting; the woman walks the floor; she has a pain, they prepare for delivery; she has a huge pain, and we dissolve from the house—three minutes.

There are only fifteen words spoken during these six minutes.

And the mood, scene, and tempo of editing does not change. We

Gleaners at the warehouses picking up fallen vegetables. From The Fight for Life.

have a time lapse, then suddenly we show our doctors again in masks, only this time they have brought a baby to a mother; she, the baby, the family, the doctors are happy—four minutes.

In this reel, then, we have had the application of our teaching; we have shown our man learning the answers to the questions he asked; we have shown a woman in pain, and a woman relieved of it; thus, roughly, one half the reel is a prelude to birth—the other half creation, the peace of birth.

Remember, in the very last reel, we have exactly the same, for our last woman, up until the time she starts to die—at which time we return to our original death music.

But I will bring this up in logical order.

THE SICK CITY: Our intern walks out of the house happily and pauses in a filthy alley—he sees children at play—he walks to the streets—and sees the hovels of the city—Now he is not surly, enraged; or defeated.

He asks a plain question: "Why do we bring them into the world?"

Thus our lullaby, that we heard under a woman, must be a sad lullaby—the music of Indians, Negroes—any old sad race with the memory of many defeats—the music of Yucatan—of Ecuador—of Portugal—carried right out onto the city streets.

Specifically, this is what I want—that lullaby to grow into the lament of the city because if it does we now have the city of decent people; of women wanting blankets and food for their children; no more drinking meat-packers whom we heard at night: during our night walk—now we want to hear from the women and children; the decent hard-working men who ask no charity or favor, but only a chance to feed and clothe and to keep well their own blood and flesh.

Thus, the power is not a dissonance in the score; the pictures furnish the harsh, unmelodic inhuman song of the city; the music is the song of the people, and it should be orchestrated with the instruments of the people; with fiddles and guitars and accordion.

(I'll settle for one guitar and one accordion, but I want to hear not only melody, warmth and a sadness of a sick people; I want to hear the simple instruments they use to tell their ballads.)

Here is the second important musical-lyric-picture sequence. Here we walk the city by day—again the pictures on the screen will move with a monotony—long scenes with no close-ups, no details—simply one scene after another passing slowly before you, interrupted occasionally by scenes of my doctors walking those streets; with vistas of the profile of the great office buildings in the background.

The speech—or narration—is in three parts. The words will be in lyrical metre, but there are three subjects; health; food; housing—that is, he sees the children and says: "Why do we bring them into the world?"—and then points to a house and says: "There is a house in America"—and we see literally hundreds of such houses.

He walks through a market and says: "We have wheat rotting in the warehouses—" immediately the picture cuts to the back of the warehouse, where we see bums grabbing rotten vegetables out of the gutter.

Finally, we return to the houses, and we show the interiors of these slums with children going to bed, eating, being bathed in the kitchen sink, etc.—and our intern says—

"How can we keep them well—," and recites the national figures on health.

SUMMARY: The day walk in the city is five minutes.
It should grow out of the music in the house where a woman enjoyed

the profound peace of birth—but a woman who lives in a mean house—which we see—and who has, now three children—whom we see.

THE EMERGENCY CASE: The minute the intern and his teacher end their walk, they are called on an emergency case.

They drive through the city—one minute—they bring the woman to a hospital, and the intern goes to the laboratory—one minute.

Now we have the third, and final musical-narrative-picture sequence.

Thus, we start the emergency case with our night music—our 4/4, drunken, lusty city music with which we started our night walk. We drive to the steel mills, we put her in a hospital—then suddenly the lights go down—and the voice of our old doctor—we don't see him—but the voice of the doctor who told the intern the meaning of medicine after he'd finished his walk in the rain, this voice narrates over a technician running a blood test.

This test starts with a close-up of blood dropping.

The voice begins—now she is not alone. Now she is neither young nor old, rich nor poor; now she is in the hands of a thousand men who worked unknown to bring the meaning of life to the world—

Now her blood is the blood of humanity, and the servants of the people have her life in their hands.

Thus we reverse the order of the music.

We opened the picture with death and went to life—the harsh beat of neat life.

Now we went out to the steel shacks to the harsh beat of the night music, and we suddenly drop down in the laboratory to the beat of the delivery room—that blood dripping is that woman's life, just as those drums in the delivery room were that woman's heart beats.

The lights go up—our intern goes back, our doctor says they can save the child—they discuss the case, and we fade-out.

SUMMARY: After the sad song of the city, we return to the wanton, savage life of the city—

We drive through it at sunset—	one minute
Drive to hospital—	one minute
Narrate in laboratory—	three minutes
Discuss case—	one minute

Actually we lead into the narration and fade away from it. The three minutes in the laboratory are the only minutes we must prepare for, in fact, are the only minutes I care about as this whole case is an excuse to bring the history of science into the meaning of medical care.

Now we have written our whole picture, and all our music. The last case is a complete recapitulation.

Again we are in a tenement. The only difference between this tenement and the first one in which we waited for a pregnant woman to have a baby is that our intern is now a teacher—but I do not feel this should be indicated, or even attempted musically.

Thus, we repeat the music we had when we were waiting for our first woman.

This woman has a baby—thus we repeat the lullaby we had under the woman in the second tenement.

She has a hemorrhage.

We repeat, then the music under the dying woman—the music under the laboratory.

They save her.

The dawn comes up.

Thus, we repeat the song of the sick city—this time with triumphant calls; with our fiddles sweeping in counterpoint over the cellos carrying the lullaby.

Factually—we repeat the music we had under a woman waiting to have a baby.

We repeat the music we had under a woman who had a baby.

We repeat the death beat of the heart.

We go back to a triumphant lullaby as the sun comes up over the factory chimneys, and our three men drive off into a grim, sick, savage city—still fighting, and still working.

This last sequence is divided into these parts:

The woman waiting—	six minutes
The delivery; peace—	one minute
The fight for life—	eight minutes
Dawn—	two minutes

Except for the final recapitulation, all our music should have been written by the time we reach this sequence; the very reiteration of the music will help me because my scene is different but the theme remains the same.

Perhaps this is completely incomprehensible, because I have so intimately heard this music in my ears for so many months I may be writing in shorthand.

But even if it is, I think you will feel one thing, there is no place where the score suddenly rises with a great crash and dominates the picture for a brief interval, as is the custom here when they have a musical sequence in a picture.

On the contrary—whenever there is music there is a voice, which I would like to sing to the music. No matter how many men might be in the orchestra, nor how powerful the music, we simply would have to key it down in order to make it sing with the words.

I am not asking for background music. That would mean I would be foolish to ask for a score; to ask you to work with me. But the score, except for the musical rests in the middle of the picture, fits into a complete pattern. Never, however, is the score used to save the picture or to bring it to life.

The life of the picture is music.

But as it is, it would be disturbing to have a sudden burst of music— just as it would be disturbing to suddenly have the voice roaring—or to key the music down to background volume, and have only a faint score "behind" the voice.

Voice and music must come into the picture and fade-out, not in synchronization, but in volume and mood, so the audience does not know actually whether it is hearing only words, or only music, or both.

PART ONE

The EXTERIOR of a large HOSPITAL at night fades in accompanied by the sound of two drums, each in double beat, giving the effect of Heart Beats which dominate the sequence. (See "Music Instructions".) As we look up we see the name of the hospital, "CITY HOSPITAL."

A hospital CORRIDOR, with interns and nurses going by, appears, and dissolves to ANOTHER CORRIDOR past a Babies' Room, which is succeeded by a THIRD CORRIDOR outside the Delivery Room, where two interns go by. Here the "Floating Nurse" goes by in the opposite direction and turns into the Delivery Room.

In the DELIVERY ROOM, moving from left to right, the scene reveals scrub and dirty nurses, the physician Leetons, the Resident Physician, the earnest young intern, O'Donnell, and a nurse who is writing while looking at Leetons. At close range we then see the patient; then the Anesthetist, who is waiting and also looking at the doctor, as well as the Floating Nurse and the Scrub Nurse. Leetons' hands are clasped, and he is waiting and looking at the patient as they regard him.

Suddenly the patient's face is contorted with pain, and the Anesthetist quickly puts on a mask. Then she turns on the nitrous oxide, and we see her hand turning the knob of the container. Leetons, whose hands are still clasped, looks at her, then back at the patient, and turns to the solution at his left, and we see him dipping his hands in it. He withdraws his hands, lifts them over the solution pan, and steps back to the patient, his hands together, palms up.

The Floating Nurse comes in with a flask of green soap, pours the contents over Leetons' hands, and goes out. Leetons turns back to dip his hands in the solution and returns to position with clasped hands.

The Anesthetist removes the mask from the patient, and her hand is seen turning the nitrous oxide valve from 90 to 0. Leetons at the same time nods to O'Donnell, whereupon the Writing Nurse comes up behind O'Donnell and puts the ear pieces of a headscope into his ears. And lifting the edge of the drape covering the patient, he takes the fetal heart tones, the Writing Nurse timing him, looking up at the clock on the wall, as the second hand of the clock is seen revolving.

Now the nurse taps O'Donnell on the back to stop him, and he straightens up.

WRITING NURSE (*removing O'Donnell's ear pieces*). Baby's heart beat a hundred and fifty.

Leetons is in a waiting position while the patient's face is again seen to be distorted with pain. He looks up, spreads his hands, and nods to the Anesthetist, who then puts a mask over the patient's face. The Scrub Nurse now hands him a clamp for the baby's cord, and Leetons puts the used instrument into a pan at his right. He is also given scissors and a belly band. (*The baby's heart tones start up at 150, in counterpoint to the mother's at 100.*)

And now the Floating Nurse is wheeling in the baby's table, and Leetons puts the baby in. The nurse covers it with a towel and wheels the table around. We see the baby being placed in the crib, a heat crib, and being straightened by the nurse's hands.

Now the Anesthetist takes the mother's pulse. The Scrub Nurse and the Floating Nurse push the table extension in place, lift the patient's drapes, and straighten her out. While the Scrub Nurse walks to the sink with the instrument tray, the Floating Nurse carries a basin to the sink, and returns for a second pan, stepping around O'Donnell, who is looking toward the baby. Then Dr. Leetons walks to the patient's side and putting a hand under the sheet, feels her abdomen. (*The baby's heart tones fade, while the heart beat of the mother starts to speed up.*)

We see the blood pressure machine and the Anesthetist watching it as the blood pressure column goes up to 110. (*The heartbeat now goes from 100 to 140.*) Suddenly the blood pressure column drops to below 40, and the patient's eyes close.

> ANESTHETIST (*jumping up*). Blood pressure sixty over forty.

Leetons seizes the patient's arm to take the pulse, and the three nurses come in close to the table.

> LEETONS (*barking at the Floating Nurse*). Half cc. of adrenalin. (*Turning to the Scrub Nurse*) Stethoscope. (*Turning to O'Donnell*) Lower her head.

We see the nurses taking out a stethoscope and injection instruments from the instrument cupboard.

The Anesthetist sits down and puts the oxygen mask on the patient. The Anesthetist's hand now turns the oxygen valve to the right, and the oxygen dial goes up to 15.

When the Scrub Nurse brings Leetons the stethoscope, he puts it on and listens to the heart, while the Floating Nurse hands the hypodermic, cotton, and adrenalin to O'Donnell, who administers the adrenalin.

> LEETONS (*looking up at the Scrub Nurse*). Get me an ampule of coramine. (*Nodding to the Anesthetist, who starts to turn the oxygen valve, while O'Donnell takes the patient's right wrist*) More oxygen!

The oxygen dial is seen going from 15 to 23.

The Scrub Nurse brings coramine, and Leetons administers it in the patient's left arm. Then he listens again to the patient's heart with the stethoscope, while O'Donnell is taking the pulse. Now O'Donnell puts the hand under the drape and looks at Leetons, everybody in the room looking tensely. Then Leetons straightens up, slowly takes out the ear pieces of his stethoscope, and turns away. The Anesthetist takes off her mask, and O'Donnell looks at the patient. Then her face is seen at close range, and it is evident that she is dead.

O'Donnell stands on the far side of the table, looking at the face of the dead woman, and his hands slowly rise. He pulls the string of his mask, and the mask falls down. He continues looking at the patient, whose dead face is seen again for an instant before a sheet is drawn over it.

The Scrub Nurse is now putting the sheet on the face, O'Donnell still staring at the dead woman, when an Orderly pushes in a cart to the head of the patient's table and lifts her on to the cart with the assistance of the nurses. Then he and the Scrub Nurse wheel it out of the room. O'Donnell hesitates, takes one step forward, and slowly follows them out of the room.

The corpse, on the cart, is pushed down the CORRIDOR outside the delivery room, O'Donnell coming out of the room and following the cart. Then O'Donnell appears in the RECEPTION ROOM or front hall while people are coming in and out, and are looking about.

NURSE. Good evening, Dr. O'Donnell.

But O'Donnell walks out without replying, and a moment later he is on the FRONT STEPS of the hospital, pausing before he walks down into the rainy night. He stops under a lamp on the street corner, and then walks away.

O'DONNELL. And now she is dead . . . Now her striving body, that brought a life into the world, is cold and empty . . .
(*O'Donnell is walking past the lighted shop windows on Michigan Boulevard.*)
Now her blood, that was bringing heat and life to them, is turning from red to purple . . .

A gleaner on her way home from the food warehouses. From The Fight for Life.

A well-developed white female of thirty—
There was no indication of cardiac trouble during labor—
Following a spontaneous delivery her pulse became rapid and her
blood pressure dropped suddenly . . .
(*He is on Rush Street now, the rain still pouring.*)
Cause of death is certified to have been acute heart failure.
Contributing cause: mitral stenosis and pregnancy.
(*He is stopped by the traffic at a crossing, but continues slowly on.*)
Acute heart failure—
But there were seven of us—
Was there one balanced second when we could have held the life
flowing from her . . . ?
(*Now he is on State Street.*)
Maybe the record was filled in—in advance . . .
She was born and lived and created a life and tonight she's dead in a
hospital basement . . .

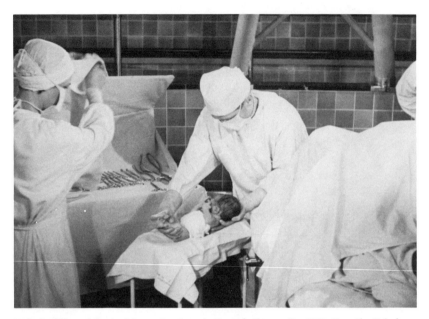

Birth of a baby and death of the mother, Lying In Hospital, Chicago, May 1939. From The Fight for Life.

(*The Hospital driveway appears as he returns from his walk. An ambulance clangs by.*)
But when . . . at what sudden signal did the complex organism of her life start to fail . . .
Maybe there's a design . . .
An eye for an eye, a tooth for a tooth . . . a life for a life . . .
Perhaps there is a design. (*He goes through the Doctor's Entrance.*)

The scene now dissolves to the HEAD DOCTOR'S OFFICE: The Head Doctor is sitting at a desk and O'Donnell is in a chair beside him, listening to him.

THE HEAD DOCTOR. An eye for an eye, a tooth for a tooth, a life for a life—Perhaps there is a design, but we don't know it. We stumble and search and sometimes think we see light—then it's dark again.

(*Turning to O'Donnell*) As biologists we know that death is not the inevitable consequence of life . . . the *stuff* of life has never died since it began. . . . But that's cold comfort for a husband in the waiting room; or a child who has lost the love of flesh and blood.

No, I cannot disclose a pattern of life and death for you, O'Donnell. But I know this, we can't learn too much about the *business* of bringing life into the world. (*Leaning forward toward the desk*) Tonight you have lost a patient. Perhaps she could have been saved. Perhaps she couldn't. Of all ailments, heart disease is the one that blows out the candle most often. (*Taking his glasses off*) But if you want to learn: if you want to be sure, there is nothing in all medicine and surgery that requires broader knowledge than obstetrics.

Too many have thought too long that having children is a normal process. It should be. In modern times it isn't. Of course, among insects it's normal for the female to die after reproduction. The salmon dies spawning. Floods and erosions are normal in nature. Perhaps *human* erosion *is* normal. Too many still think so. . . .

The damnable thing is—where are you youngsters going to learn? (*Rising and walking toward the window, his glasses in his right hand*) Right now, for all these grand clinics, 90% of our babies are brought by men with 5% training. We don't open up our science to enough men—only four out of fifty of your class will get a residence in a hospital. (*Turning and coming back to the desk*) There is a place—(*Sitting down at the desk, gesturing toward the window*)— there in the slums where two young doctors are bringing modern science to the poor women of the city . . . if you want to start over, and work as you've never worked before . . . if you want to learn, and to teach as you learn . . . there is a place.

With these words, the scene fades out.

PART TWO

A STREET under a cloudy sky fades in. It is day, and a man is then seen running across the street into a saloon.

There are two customers at the bar in the SALOON as the Man runs in from the street and heads for a booth. Here he puts a nickel in the phone and dials a number.

At once we see the exterior of the MATERNITY CENTER, women going into it; and this dissolves to a view of the Center's SWITCH-

BOARD ROOM where the receptionist and switchboard girl, Effie, is at her desk.

EFFIE. Maternity Center . . . Maternity Center . . . Has she had a baby or is she having a baby?

In the BAG ROOM, seen next, two nurses are packing doctors' bags. One of them turns, leaving packing, and goes to the bag shelves.

EFFIE'S VOICE. What is the name, please? Doran. D-O-R-A-N. Address, please. Four-o-five-six Fulton. (*The bags in the* BAG ROOM *are seen at close range on a shelf.*) Has your wife been coming to the Center? Fine . . . is she having pains? When did the pains start? How often are they coming? (*Hands take a normal pair of bags off the shelf.*) Has she had any children before? Now you collect some newspapers. Stacks of newspapers. (*A nurse is seen taking the bags out of the bag room.*) Get two clean kettles and put some water on to boil. Be sure the kettles have covers. (*The nurse is now placing bags on the table in the* BULLETIN BOARD ROOM.) Do you have any oilcloth in the house? Olive oil? Now don't you worry, the doctor will be right over.

In the BULLETIN BOARD ROOM, Dr. Leetons enters from the switchboard door, picks up a prenatal record from a desk, and goes over toward the bulletin board.

EFFIE'S VOICE. Maternity Center. . . . Maternity Center . . .

We get a close view of the BULLETIN BOARD. Here Leetons starts to write his case up. As he finishes writing the name and address, he looks over his shoulder. (We see the CLOCK registering 11:26.) Leetons chalks up the time and the names of the crew.

Another physician, Paul, and the nurse, Miss Holtz, enter. Miss Holtz, stopping at a desk, punches a card in the time clock. Paul goes over to the table and picks up a bag. Leetons, coming from the right, picks up his bag and leaves, followed by Paul and the nurse.

Leetons enters the SWITCHBOARD ROOM, followed by Paul and Holtz. He stops at the switchboard as they go past him.

EFFIE'S VOICE. Maternity Center. . . . Maternity Center . . .

Effie, at the switchboard, tears off a slip of paper on which she has been writing and hands it to Leetons, whose hand is seen holding it.

EFFIE. It's south of Lincoln Park, doctor.

Leetons glances at the slip of paper in his hand, puts it in his pocket, and looks up.

EFFIE'S VOICE. Maternity Center . . . Maternity Center. . . . Has she had a baby or is she having a baby?

Paul finishes marking his crew out and the next two up. Holtz watching him, they turn.

EFFIE'S VOICE. What is the name please? Address? Twelve-fifty-one Monroe Avenue.

Leetons nods, puts on his hat, and goes down the steps, followed by Paul and Holtz.

EFFIE'S VOICE. Is your wife having pains? How often are the pains coming? Has she had any children before? Now you collect some newspapers—stacks of newspapers. Get two clean kettles and put some water on to boil. Be sure the kettles have covers. Do you have any oil cloth in the house—olive oil?

Outside the MATERNITY CENTER, Leetons, Holtz and Paul come out the door, down the steps, turn, and start walking toward Maxwell Street, while Effie's Voice, fading, repeats, "Maternity Center . . . Maternity Center."

A woman goes into the building, the lettering over the door reading "MATERNITY CENTER," as the music and the heart beats rise in volume and Effie's Voice fades out.

When this scene dissolves, a SCROLL, entitled "Rules for Pregnant Women," unwinds, giving the rules on clothing and diet, and other information. Then we see, first the WAITING ROOM, full of women; then the SOCIAL SECURITY ROOM, where two women are being questioned by two interns. We see the FIRST INTERN filling out a record; then a SECOND INTERN doing likewise; then a SOCIAL SECURITY WORKER, working at a desk.

FIRST INTERN. Has there been any sickness in your family?

PATIENT. No.

FIRST INTERN. Any cancer?

PATIENT. No.

FIRST INTERN. Tuberculosis?

PATIENT. No.

FIRST INTERN. Diabetes?

PATIENT. No.

FIRST INTERN. Kidney trouble?

PATIENT. No.

FIRST INTERN. Heart trouble?

PATIENT. No.

SECOND INTERN (*who comes into view along with his patient*). Is the entrance in the front or in the rear?

PATIENT. Rear.

SECOND INTERN. What floor?

PATIENT. Third.

SECOND INTERN. Have you a telephone?

PATIENT. No.

SECOND INTERN. What's the name of your closest relative?

PATIENT. George Fenning.

SECOND INTERN. How many children have you now?

PATIENT. Three.

SECOND INTERN. Have any of them been ill recently?

PATIENT. No.

Now the EXAMINATION ROOM appears—after a brief view of a LABORATORY with a nurse and technician. DR. BALLOU is examining a patient, MRS. ALSON, touching her abdomen in order to determine the position of the baby.

BALLOU. About how many months pregnant would you say she is, doctor?

As a larger part of the room appears, O'Donnell is seen beside Ballou, holding the record, while a nurse is in attendance and Ballou's associate, Dr. Hanson, is washing his hands at the sink.

O'DONNELL. About seven months.

BALLOU. Could you hear the baby's heart beats?

O'DONNELL. Yes, sir.

Ballou takes the record from O'Donnell, looks at it, frowns, and pulls at his ear.

BALLOU. Teeth, throat, heart, lungs—Blood pressure a hundred and forty over ninety.

The view contracting, we now see Ballou and his patient—Ballou looking at the record, not really paying attention to Mrs. Alson, who is looking up at him. Then Hanson, drying his hands, walks a step or two toward the table.

BALLOU. Mrs. Alson has been having headaches every day.

MRS. ALSON. Almost every morning.

Ballou and Hanson exchange looks. Ballou hands the record to O'Donnell and examines Mrs. Alson's wrists and ankles.

BALLOU. Is your husband working, Mrs. Alson?

MRS. ALSON. Two days a week.

BALLOU. Have you someone to help you with the housework?

MRS. ALSON. My sister comes in once in a while, but it's hard for her to get away.

Ballou steps back toward Mrs. Alson's head, looks at her reassuringly, and starts to help her up. O'Donnell and the nurse step forward and do it for him, the latter holding drapes around the patient now sitting on the examination table.

Myron McCormick as the young intern in The Fight for Life.

BALLOU. Do you feel sick at your stomach—or dizzy sometimes?

MRS. ALSON. No, sir.

BALLOU. You can dress now.

The Nurse helps Mrs. Alson down from the table, and they go out.

O'Donnell goes over to the desk with the record and sits down as the nurse from the other examination room sticks her head in the doorway.

NURSE. We're ready in here now, Doctor Hanson.

HANSON. Coming right away.

BALLOU. I'm glad you called me. You were right.

HANSON. I knew you would want to see her, Ballou.

As Hanson goes into the other room, Ballou comes over to O'Donnell, who is sitting at the desk writing in the record.

BALLOU (*leaning over*). Mark in red ink: "Patient is toxic and to watch for pre-eclampsia." Make sure she comes in once a week for blood pressure. If she doesn't come, send for her. Now, doctor, what were the symptoms?

O'DONNELL (*turning and rising, reading from the record*). She was a few pounds overweight—her test showed a slight trace of albumen. She had a slight rise in blood pressure.

BALLOU (*pointing at the record*). She had a *sudden* rise in blood pressure—and then there were the headaches.

O'DONNELL (*rising, taking the record, and arguing as* BALLOU *starts to go into the laboratory*). But, doctor, wouldn't that mean just as well that she might have kidney trouble, or bad diet, or that she might be a hyper-thyroid?

BALLOU (*washing his hands, taking off his gloves first*). If it were kidney trouble, she likely would have had high blood pressure from the very beginning. If she were a hyper-thyroid, we would find many symptoms besides high blood pressure. We don't know much about these toxemias of pregnancy, doctor. We know that men don't have eclampsia, and women who aren't pregnant never have it. (*Turning and drying his hands*) We do know that twenty-five per cent of the women who die having children or in pregnancy, die from eclampsia. And they could be saved. If we didn't heed these danger signals we found, at any time the patient might have an eclamptic seizure— stabs of light before the eyes—convulsions—and then it's a little late for diagnosis.

Ballou is at the stand wiping his hands, O'Donnell facing him, as Mrs. Alson and the nurse enter, Ballou and O'Donnell turning to them. The nurse goes out and returns with a card, and hands it to Ballou.

Mrs. Alson and the nurse turn and go out through the doors. Ballou throws his apron in a hamper and goes to the closed door for his coat and hat, while O'Donnell moves to the stand to wash his hands. As Ballou puts on his coat, the nurse from the examination room comes in and signals to them to come to another case in a second examination room. O'Donnell nods, but turns back to face Ballou who hasn't finished yet.

BALLOU. These are the three things that kill mothers, doctor. Remember them—eclampsia—infection—hemorrhage.

And now—after glimpses of women entering the MATERNITY CENTER—we are in the SECOND EXAMINATION ROOM, where O'Donnell is leaning over a patient on a table, counting the baby's heartbeats as a nurse holds a watch. Following this, we are back in the FIRST EXAMINATION ROOM, where Hanson is examining another patient's eyes with a flashlight, O'Donnell watching and learning more. Hanson gives the flashlight to O'Donnell, who makes the tests also. Hanson then holds the patient's head and extends his right forefinger up in the air. Bringing his finger down toward the patient's nose, he releases her head and looks across at O'Donnell.

The nurse crosses to the instrument table, taking the flashlight from O'Donnell. She picks up the blood pressure apparatus and hands it to O'Donnell, who takes the patient's blood pressure and then straightens up, unwrapping the apparatus as Hanson feels the patient's right eye below the lower lid. The nurse takes the blood pressure apparatus, sets it down, and walks off left, Hanson looking after her. Then she brings the tray and stands at the head of the table as Hanson takes cotton from the tray and wipes the patient's ear.

We see a HAND jabbing a needle into the ear; then the Nurse handing O'Donnell a bottle or jar. Hanson takes a pipette from the tray, sucks blood from the patient's ear, then takes the jar from O'Donnell; he sucks in the solution, winds the tubing around his finger, shakes the pipette, then puts the pipette down on the tray as the nurse hands Hanson a slide. Then we see blood from the ear being put on the slide; and after this, O'Donnell handing another slide to Hanson, who makes the smear on the first slide with it. He puts the slides down on the tray and wipes the patient's ear with cotton. The nurse takes the tray out. O'Donnell looks at the patient as Hanson fixes the drape and smiles at her; then he looks at Hanson, who turns and goes out, O'Donnell following him.

In the LABORATORY ROOM: Hanson and O'Donnell enter from the first Examination Room, O'Donnell with the record. Hanson goes over to wash his hands, while O'Donnell goes to the bench with the record and pen. We see the nurse's hands passing the blood test tray to the laboratory technician, a woman.

BALLOU (*to O'Donnell*). Now, doctor, did you find anything unusual in this case?

O'DONNELL (*at the bench*). Her blood pressure is normal. She has no cardiac trouble, but she complains of shortness of breath. She's pallid.

Hanson walks to the technician, who is bent over a microscope and is writing with a pencil on a pad, figuring the red count. He picks up the slip of paper with the blood count. The technician starts to fill the haemoglobin tube with solution as Hanson looks over her shoulder—meanwhile speaking to O'Donnell.

HANSON. Note that she is to come in every two weeks for a checkup.

Hanson has seen the amount of solution poured in by the technician to dilute the color of the blood to match the others. The technician is holding the haemometer up to the light.

HANSON (*nodding, seeing that the colors match*). Haemoglobin fifty per cent count, three million, two hundred thousand red blood cells—(*Putting down the paper with the blood count, and starting towards O'Donnell's bench*) Our patient is anemic—probably over-worked and underfed. (*Taking O'Donnell's pen and writing out a prescription*) We'll give her sixty grams of iron pills daily—and try to get her some fresh vegetables. (*Straightening up and looking at O'Donnell*) You must watch this patient carefully, doctor. (*As we watch O'Donnell at close range, listening*) Remember your Bible, doctor; the blood is the life; hemorrhage in these cases often proves fatal.

This scene dissolves to a series of rapid scenes (that is, a MONTAGE) of WOMEN—of feet coming into view; of clothes going off and on; a patient's back. Then, in the first EXAMINATION ROOM, after a glimpse of another patient's face, Ballou is seen listening through a stethoscope to this patient's heart. The nurse stands by the patient's head holding a record with a cardiac sheet clipped to it, while O'Donnell stands looking at the patient. Ballou listens to the heart in three positions, following which the nurse helps the woman sit up.

Now Ballou finishes his heart examination on the woman's back, after which O'Donnell and the nurse lower the patient.

The nurse hands her records to Ballou and goes off right to get a towel. Ballou studies the cardiac action, then hands the record to O'Donnell and palpates the patient's throat.

Ballou takes the towel from the nurse and wipes off the makeup from the patient's lips. This done, he examines them for cyanosis.

Next Ballou takes the patient's left hand from under the drape and feels the first three fingers. He moves the hand over to O'Donnell, who also feels the fingers, bending over while the woman's face is looking at him. Ballou replaces the woman's arm at her side, and the nurse hands the record to Ballou and helps the woman sit up.

Now it is night and the SWITCHBOARD fades in as Effie is plugging in for a call.

> EFFIE. Maternity Center . . . Maternity Center. . . . Oh, yes, Doctor Craig. Doctor Ballou is busy right now. I'll give him the message . . . Yes, Doctor Hanson is busy, too. . . .

And then we move, right to left, from Effie to the door, and into the WAITING ROOM, where Dr. Ballou is standing beside a chair and table under a projection screen. Hanson is rising from his chair, but when Ballou smiles at him, Hanson sits down and crosses his legs. Ballou begins his speech easily, becoming serious immediately, while the scene discloses interns and students listening.

> BALLOU. You came to the Maternity Center, from all over the country, because you wished to learn more about obstetrics. (*As the students are seen listening*) Your experience for the most part has been limited to a few months training in a general hospital. But even in that short time, you've seen tragic accidents resulting in death or injury to mothers and babies. (*As Ballou is picked out at close range*) You know some of them could have been avoided—and—(*looking pointedly at O'Donnell*)—that is why many of you are here. (*O'Donnell is seen scowling.*) We have two objectives here at the Center—to bring modern obstetrical care to the poor women of the city, and to teach you the art and science of obstetrics as practised by the best institutions in the country. (*A series of portraits of pregnant women is seen, and then Ballou is picked out again.*) As doctors, we have to face this fact: today, almost as many mothers die bringing children into the world, as did twenty-five years ago. With all the new science

and medicine we have in this country, we lose more human lives from childbearing than we do from cancer. The deaths of mothers and infants under one month ranks second only to heart disease in the total mortality figures.

You know the three things that kill mothers. Eclampsia, infection, hemorrhage. And of these, child-bed fever—infection at birth—is still the chief killer. Thirty-five out of one hundred women who die, die from infection. And most of them could have been saved. (*Nodding to the projectionist*) All right, Dan. (*Hanson rises.*)

Hanson and Ballou start back to the projection machine, and the lights go down in the Waiting Room.

(*At this point a silent film, the demonstration Dr. Ballou is giving his audience, starts. The action of this demonstration takes place in a* BEDROOM, *typical of the bedrooms in which so many women give birth.*)

As a kitchen SINK fades in, hands are seen washing in the wash stand for a long time. Then Ballou is seen washing his hands at the wash stand; and then Hanson and the nurse at the TABLE (in the middle of the room), are holding a bag each, and spreading newspapers on the table, placing the bags in proper position on top.

On one chair next to the table, Hanson and the nurse spread newspapers, and put hats and coats on the chair. The nurse and Hanson take out and put on aprons. The nurse helps Hanson unpack the sink setup, and carries part of it for him as he goes to the sink, while Ballou is still washing his hands. Hanson puts down the first newspaper on the sink, the brush and soap, and puts a glove between folds of newspaper. We now see the brush, soap, and other objects at close range on the sink.

Then the nurse hands Hanson the rectal newspaper and towel, and goes to the table to get out her stove material.

Ballou finishes washing his hands, while Hanson hangs up the towel and newspaper. The nurse at the TABLE takes pans, stacked properly for boiling over the stove, and then there is a close view of the pans on the STOVE, along with two kettles already there. The nurse takes the covers off and we see what's in the pans.

Onlookers gathering to watch camera crew film a street scene for The Fight for Life,
Chicago, May 1939.

At the TABLE Hanson, standing with Ballou, is rolling a stack of newspapers, the hands soon seen at close range separately. The paper rolled,
Ballou helps Hanson wrap it in the outside sheet and fold it properly.
The nurse enters, takes blood pressure machine, heart and head stetho-
scopes over to the bed, and places them on the newspaper-covered table
at the head of the bed, hanging the head stethoscope over the newspaper-covered railing of the bed. The bed already has clean sheets and
coverings. The stool next to the bed is already covered with newspaper.

Hanson and Ballou come to the BED, carrying rolls of paper and an
ironing board. As the nurse leaves the bed area they put the ironing
board under the bed; and when the nurse comes over with oil cloth and
pins, they spread them on the bed.

The scene shows the three making the bed setup—placing the rolls
under the oil cloth and pinning the oil cloth down, followed by a close
view of Ballou's and Hanson's hands at work.

The nurse, now in cap and mask, brings pans and places them on the
newspaper-covered STOOL next to the bed. She drops tablets of bi-

Dudley Digges as the old doctor. From The Fight for Life.

chloride of mercury in one and Lysol into the other. The bichloride and the Lysol are seen dissolving in the pans.

At the SINK again, now set up properly, Ballou is in the midst of scrubbing up, while Hanson is putting on mask and cap. Ballou scrubs as far as the elbows.

Now Ballou has finished scrubbing up and as he moves over to dip his hands into the pan of Lysol on the drainboard, the nurse comes to the wash basin and drains water from the plate-covered pan. Then the nurse brings the pan and the plate from the sink to the bed, placing them on the foot of the bed, the plate now on the bottom. As Ballou and Hanson come toward the bed, the nurse takes the pan off the plate, and Ballou starts a glove demonstration—the hands, seen closely, putting on the gloves.

Then, after glimpses of the sink and the stove properly set up, ready for the delivery, and of the table with bags and baby setup, the view moves to the bed with Hanson, Ballou and the nurse in positions for the delivery.

Now, at the TABLE, Ballou holds scales with a baby wrapped in a blanket, hanging on scales—Hanson holding one hand under the baby to show how it should be supported. The nurse is pouring olive oil into a saucer. This is followed by close views of the baby setup on the pillow; and the setup between the bags—olive oil now in the saucer with a bottle beside it, and pelvimeter; everything except the scales which Ballou is holding.

At the STOVE the nurse is now putting pans on to boil. And before she covers the last pan we get a close view of the instruments and gloves about to be boiled.

At the TABLE Hanson and Ballou take off masks and caps. Hanson sits down with the record, Ballou leaning over him. The last page of the RECORD comes to view—the last line reading, "Tell what you could have done better and what to do the next time." At this point in the film demonstration, we again find Ballou and Hanson at the projection machine.

BALLOU. This washing and scrubbing up may seem like old stuff to you, but we're fanatics here on the subject. Remember infection 'most always comes from outside. A clean pair of hands is your guard against invisible death.

When you arrive at your home, keep everything above table level at least. Newspapers are the cleanest coverings we find in these poor houses. Spread them on the kitchen table and on chairs. You're carrying those bags and wearing your clothes from home to home, and you must guard against carrying infection with you.

Put the large bag on the right and the small one on the left. Get used to making every operation systematic. You may have to find those bags in the dark some night—in a hurry.

Here we don't have sterile sheets, and sterile surgical tables and the white aseptic-looking furnishings of a hospital room, that too often make a doctor careless because he feels secure. You can see the dirt where you're going.

In three years our students and nurses here delivered 9,000 mothers without losing one from infection. You have to maintain that high standard. Only the insides of the basins, the instruments, your hands and the obstetrical area are sterile—.

You scrub carefully for ten minutes, but there's still a danger of contamination—your gloves are specially folded so they can be slipped on without the outside of the glove ever touching the skin. You wear two pairs of gloves at the beginning of delivery—the outer pair is removed following the preparation of the patient, and if your sterile gloves get within a foot of anything, you can just *assume* they're contaminated.

Of course, we don't recommend a complete return to deliveries in the home. The isolated, well-equipped, maternity hospital is the ideal place for a mother to have a baby. But we're not dealing with ideal conditions—the facts are that over half the women who had babies last year had them at home. A quarter of a million of them had only a midwife to attend them. And thousands of mothers went to hospitals where there was inadequate equipment, or men without obstetrical training.

We want to give you a technique that will enable you to go into a hospital or into private practice able to meet any condition you may find there.

You have one broad plan on a case—to bring a live baby to a live uninjured mother. You have created an island of safety against death from infection. You will remain with your patient until at least two hours after the baby is born, and until you've filled in carefully a complete record of your case.

This is followed by quick views of the students' faces looking at the movie; of the screen with backs of the students' heads; of Ballou and Hanson still standing beside the projection machine, talking.

Finally the door opens and Effie enters, and hands a note to Ballou, who looks at it and puts it in his coat pocket, while one intern sitting in the back row gets up and goes out.

Then, after another glimpse of the students looking at the screen, the lights go up in the room, and the projectionist starts to take down the machine. Students twist around in their chairs, as Ballou looks at his watch.

BALLOU. Since we have been in this room two mothers have had babies—somewhere in this country—and died.

One of them might have been saved.

Remember, gentlemen, it is not only pathological knowledge and a skill with your hands that makes a great obstetrician, it is vigilance, vigilance, eternal vigilance—one that does not let you forget for one tragic moment that during pregnancy and labor you have in your hands the lives of two people.———Dismissed.

In the WAITING ROOM (it is night), the interns and students are breaking up into little groups.

BALLOU. I had a call from Dr. Craig. Think I had better go over there right away.

The students file out as one STUDENT goes over to Hanson.

FIRST STUDENT. Doctor, I can't understand why you don't include Stander's low reserve kidney in your toxemia classification.

A SECOND STUDENT comes over to Ballou.

SECOND STUDENT. I'd like to have seen that Caesarian you did with Dr. Johnson—we were out on a case.

BALLOU. I'll try to remember to call you next time.

Then O'DONNELL and a THIRD STUDENT are picked out.

THIRD STUDENT. Coming upstairs, O'Donnell?

O'DONNELL. No, I think I'll get a cup of coffee.

The third student leaves as Hanson stops O'Donnell.

HANSON. All through with your books, eh, Doctor?

O'DONNELL. Yeah.

HANSON. We'll see.

O'Donnell exits as Hanson glances at Ballou. They turn and go out.

PART THREE

The STUDENT BOARD ROOM fades in by day, and we see O'Donnell writing up the list of the Hanson crew on the "Mendez case." We then follow him as he turns, puts the record in his pocket, and walks toward the bag table.

EFFIE'S VOICE. Maternity Center . . . Maternity Center . . . Maternity Center . . . Maternity Center . . . Maternity Center. . . . Has she had a baby or is she having a baby?

What is the name, please. . . . Mendez. M-E-N-D-E-Z. Address? One-two-seven East Jay Street.

Has your wife been coming to the Center? Fine. . . . Is she having pains? When did the pains start . . . how often are they coming? Has she had any children before? . . . Now you collect some newspapers . . . stacks of newspapers. . . . Get two clean kettles and put some water on to boil. Be sure the kettles have covers. Do you have any oil cloth in the house? . . . Olive oil? . . . Fine. . . . Now don't you worry. The doctor will be right over.

Hanson, O'Donnell and Miss Horn come out of the bulletin board room to the SWITCHBOARD. O'Donnell and Miss Horn are going to the Intern's Board, Hanson stopping at the switchboard, where Effie hands him an address on a card.

EFFIE. It's one-twenty-seven East Jay Street. The entrance is in the rear, Doctor.

Hanson takes the paper and looks at O'Donnell.

HANSON. Now, doctor, do you have your stethoscope?

O'DONNELL. Yes, sir.

HANSON. Record?

O'DONNELL. Yes, sir.

HANSON. Flash light?

O'DONNELL. Yes, sir.

HANSON. All right. Let's go.

They go out.

OUTSIDE the Maternity Center Hanson, O'Donnell, and Miss Horn come down the steps out of the door, and get into a car. The car backs up, turns right and then around the corner left down MAXWELL ST.

The car comes down Maxwell St., and turns right at the end of the block. It goes through FIVE SLUM STREETS; then into DEARBORN STREET, Hanson's crew seen in the car; then it comes under an "L" and slows down in front of a HOUSE.

The crew gets out, Hanson goes upstairs to look at the house number, then comes down and goes around the steps into an ALLEY, followed by O'Donnell and Miss Horn. Then the Hanson crew goes through the alley, walks along the back of the house, and starts up three flights of STAIRS. We see the crew climbing, until they reach the top and Hanson knocks at a door.

The scene dissolves to the MENDEZ KITCHEN where the knocking on the door is heard. A girl, Elsie Mendez, opens the door, and Hanson and his crew enter the room, in which we see the pantry, sink, and stove. A doorway leads into a bedroom in which the patient, Mrs. Mendez, is in bed.

HANSON. Hello, we're the doctors.

Elsie brings newspapers which Miss Horn and Hanson take from her, Hanson saying "Thank you," and spread on the table and the chair. Now Hanson and O'Donnell put down their bags, take off their coats, and roll up their sleeves. Then Hanson, followed by Miss Horn and O'Donnell, moves toward the bedroom. Mrs. Mendez is lying in bed as the crew enters the BEDROOM, a very dirty room, with clothes hanging out of a cupboard on the left. Miss Horn removes a shoe and a doll from the floor, placing them on the cupboard. Then she comes back with newspapers which she places on the bed for Hanson to sit on.

HANSON (*sitting on the bed*). How are you feeling, Mrs. Mendez?

MRS. MENDEZ. A little pain.

HANSON (*turning to O'Donnell, who turns and goes out*). All right. (*As Miss Horn also leaves, he turns back to the patient*). Have you been sick since we saw you last? Have any members of your family been sick? (*As she shakes her head, he gets up and goes out.*)

In the KITCHEN: Miss Horn has come in, followed by O'Donnell. They go over to the table. Miss Horn opens a big bag, O'Donnell a little one. They take out aprons and put them on. The girls, Elsie and Tillie, go into the bedroom.

Miss Horn goes to the sink, clears rubbish off and puts it on top of the stove. O'Donnell unpacks the wash setup. Miss Horn washes her hands, while O'Donnell takes out instruments and records.

Then Miss Horn goes into the bedroom, followed by Elsie. Hanson, seen through the door, looks toward the children, Elsie and Tillie, who now go, hand in hand, into a second bedroom and close the door. O'Donnell, left alone, is now at the SINK washing his hands. Cockroaches are running across the sink; O'Donnell disposes of them; and goes on washing.

Hanson, seen in the bedroom through the door, comes into the kitchen, and puts on an apron at the table.

HANSON. Give her a physical examination.

O'DONNELL. Yes, sir.

Hanson takes the rectal setup over to the sink as O'Donnell goes to the table, puts down his towel, takes up instruments, and goes into the bedroom. Hanson puts up a towel and newspaper and starts washing his hands.

O'Donnell enters the BEDROOM as Miss Horn is struggling with a teetering cupboard. He sets the instruments on a chair and gives the newspaper to Miss Horn to put under the leg of the cupboard and Miss Horn steadies it.

O'Donnell takes a newspaper from the stool and Miss Horn spreads it on the cupboard. O'Donnell puts paper over the back of the bed, and hangs his stethoscope over it. Miss Horn puts a sheet over Mrs. Mendez, takes pulse, and removes the thermometer from her mouth. O'Donnell starts to take the blood pressure, while Miss Horn starts writing in the record.

O'Donnell, having finished the blood pressure, pulls out the ear pieces of a stethoscope and looks toward Miss Horn.

O'DONNELL. Hundred and twenty-four over eighty.

Miss Horn takes the blood pressure machine and gives O'Donnell the stethoscope. O'Donnell takes the fetal heart tones, Miss Horn timing them.

MISS HORN (*tapping his hands*). They are one fifty.

O'Donnell straightens up, and takes off the head stethoscope. Miss Horn puts it on the cupboard and gives him the heart stethoscope.

In the KITCHEN Hanson at the sink is putting on a rectal glove. Then he starts toward the bedroom door.

In the BEDROOM, O'Donnell listens to the patient's heart, finishes the examination, and starts toward the dresser. Miss Horn takes the baby setup from the side cupboard and leaves as Hanson comes in, sits down, and gets ready to start the rectal examination.

In the KITCHEN Miss Horn puts the pans on to boil, and very soon they are steaming. Miss Horn starts the baby setup between the two bags. When she finishes, she goes into the bedroom. As she does this, Hanson and O'Donnell come out of the bedroom, and go to the sink.

> HANSON (*washing his gloved hand*). Our plan of delivery here is simple, doctor. She has a normal pelvis. Her pains are weak and we may have to help her. We shouldn't have any trouble. Fill out the record.

As O'Donnell goes to the table, Hanson crosses over and looks over his shoulder.

In the BEDROOM, Miss Horn helps the patient up.

Then Mrs. Mendez enters the KITCHEN from the bedroom, and starts to pick up the coffee pot on the stove. Hanson comes and stops her, O'Donnell brings in a chair.

> HANSON (*helping her into the chair*). Are you comfortable, Mother?

> MRS. MENDEZ (*seen closely*). Yes, I am.

Mrs. Mendez fingers baby clothes as Hanson walks to the sink and O'Donnell goes into the bedroom.

In the BEDROOM, Miss Horn and O'Donnell do the bed setup. Then O'Donnell exits.

Following this we see O'Donnell in the KITCHEN, telephoning his report to the Center; and at the SWITCHBOARD in the MATERNITY CENTER, as an intern and a student and a nurse come in, returning from a case, and as the crew goes to the bag room, the phone rings.

EFFIE (*taking the call*). Yes, Doctor O'Donnell. Fetal heart tones one fifty. Station minus one. Pains moderate—every ten minutes. All right, doctor, I have that.

A nurse comes in, takes the slip Effie has written on and handed to her and goes to the Bulletin Board Room.

In the BULLETIN BOARD ROOM, now, the nurse chalks up O'Donnell's report on the board. The scene then dissolves back to the MENDEZ KITCHEN, at night, where Hanson is now reading next to the table. Mrs. Mendez walks into the kitchen, looks at the clock on the stove, walks out, walks in again, and moves the clock to look at it.

Hanson is seen looking toward her, and his eyes follow her as she starts to go out again. She walks out, leaving Hanson reading.

In the BEDROOM, Miss Horn is seated at the foot of the bed, and O'Donnell is asleep in the chair. Mrs. Mendez walks toward the bed, turns and walks back toward the kitchen, and walks toward the bed again. She looks at a picture over the bed as she turns. Miss Horn looks at her watch, timing the pain. The Patient walks toward the kitchen and back again, looking at O'Donnell in the chair, while Miss Horn looks at her watch again. The woman walks back and forth twice more; five times in all.

In the KITCHEN, with O'Donnell viewed in the background, Hanson is at the table. Mrs. Mendez comes into the kitchen, looks at the clock, starts to take it down, and has a terrific labor pain. She clutches the stove. We see her closely as the pains come.

Hanson looks at her, sets down his book, and goes over and holds her, timing the pain. Then he starts to take her into the bedroom.

In the BEDROOM, O'Donnell is asleep and Miss Horn is on the bed as Hanson enters with Mrs. Mendez.

HANSON. Scrub up, doctor!

O'Donnell gets up, rubbing his eyes, and goes into the kitchen as Hanson and Horn help Mrs. Mendez into the bed.

O'Donnell comes into the KITCHEN, rubbing his eyes, and goes to the sink, where he scrubs up. Hanson puts on his mask and goes out.

Hanson returns to the BEDROOM, takes the patient's right hand, and glances out toward the kitchen as Horn enters with pans.

O'Donnell is finishing his scrubbing up in the KITCHEN. He turns to dip his hands in Lysol. His hands are seen going through the solution.

Then O'Donnell brings his hands out of the solution and starts off right.

In the BEDROOM, Hanson is holding the patient's right arm. O'Donnell enters with wet arms held high. Horn crosses left to right, uncovers the plate with the gloves. O'Donnell shakes out the gloves and starts putting them on. He finishes putting on a second pair of gloves, and Horn puts a headscope over his cap. Horn goes left, and pulls back the drape on the woman, and O'Donnell bends to take the fetal heart tones. In doing so he loses his balance and puts his right hand on Mrs. Mendez' shoulder.

Hanson taps O'Donnell's left shoulder and O'Donnell looks up. Hanson points to O'Donnell's hand on Mrs. Mendez' shoulder.

HANSON (*as O'Donnell straightens up*). The hand, doctor.

O'Donnell looks at his hand guiltily, and Miss Horn comes in and takes off his outer glove before he goes back to continue the fetal heart tones. Mrs. Mendez has another pain and clutches Hanson's right arm tightly.

The scene dissolves to the Maternity Center SWITCHBOARD, where Effie takes the call. Effie is writing on a slip of paper as a nurse comes in. She takes the slip from Effie as the latter takes another call and walks to the Bulletin Board room.

In the BULLETIN BOARD ROOM, we hear:

EFFIE'S VOICE. Has she had a baby, or is she having a baby?

Then we see a nurse's HAND on the Bulletin Board as she wipes off the last report on the O'Donnell case and writes: "Delivered O.K. (Female 6½ lbs. T.P.R. Normal)." The board becomes a scroll and rolls slowly through a series of cases, ending on the nurse's hand writing opposite the name of O'Donnell's second case the list of the crew; then the last report before delivery.

EFFIE'S VOICE (*as the scroll rolls; repeatedly on different tone levels*). Maternity Center . . . Maternity Center. . . . Has she had a baby or is she having a baby?

PART FOUR

The previous scene dissolves to an ALLEY, seen in daylight, our vision tilting up to a second story window and to stairways rising up.

Next we see the BLAUSER KITCHEN, with Miss Holtz at the stove. Then in the BEDROOM, the curtains are drawn back by O'Donnell, and he and Ballou take off their caps and masks. O'Donnell takes out paper rolls from the bed and an ironing board from beneath the patient. He takes off leggings and rolls up the paper.

O'Donnell brings rolls and ironing board into the KITCHEN, and Miss Holtz goes into the bedroom with a wash cloth and white basin, as O'Donnell washes his face and hands. Miss Holtz, who has returned, packs the big bag and turns to help O'Donnell, who leaves with the ironing board and paper rolls. Miss Holtz picks up the wash basin and goes into the bedroom as O'Donnell turns to the sink and washes.

In the BEDROOM, Ballou straightens out the sheet as Miss Holtz enters with the wash-basin, takes the cloth, and bends over the patient. We see the patient's face and Ballou's hand with the wash cloth, wiping it clean.

Ballou finishes washing her face—turns the sheet down, examines the abdomen, and goes out, as Miss Holtz moves in to tidy her up.

Miss Holtz turns, puts the basin on a chest of drawers, turns back, removes newspaper from under the patient's right shoulder, lifts and settles her, then exits with basin and papers, and re-enters, continuing to clear up the room.

Ballou, in the KITCHEN, is finishing washing his hands. O'Donnell is seated at the table, writing on the record. Ballou dries his hands as he comes toward O'Donnell and leans over him.

BALLOU. Mark low-grade toxemia. We'll have to watch her kidneys closely.

Ballou goes back to the sink, hangs up the towel, goes to the dresser drawer, bends over it and his hand draws back the blanket and examines the baby seen lying there. With O'Donnell still at the table, Ballou then walks toward the bedroom.

BALLOU. Now the final checkup.

O'DONNELL (*looking up*). Yes, sir.

Ballou walks into the BEDROOM, puts a thermometer in the patient's mouth, and feels her pulse. O'Donnell finishes writing, gets up, takes the blood pressure machine and stethoscope, and goes into the bedroom as Ballou steps back.

O'Donnell takes the patient's blood pressure in the BEDROOM while the thermometer is still in her mouth. O'Donnell's left hand unplugs the machine, while Ballou's hand takes the thermometer from the patient's mouth. Holding the thermometer, Ballou steps back to the dresser, as O'Donnell stands up and feels the patient's abdomen. In the KITCHEN, Miss Holtz goes to the stove, removes double pans, goes to the sink, drains pans, goes to the table, wipes pans and puts them in the big bag and continues packing both bags.

Miss Holtz enters the BEDROOM with the baby in the dresser drawer. Ballou takes drawer from Holtz, puts it on the bed, and lifts the blanket.

We get a close view of the baby in the drawer, Ballou's hand holding the blanket back from its face. He replaces the blanket and moves the drawer up near the mother. O'Donnell helps her to raise herself to look at the baby, then helps her back again.

Mr. Blauser enters and goes to the bedroom door with their children, James and Roger, while O'Donnell folds up the equipment.

BALLOU (*looking toward the doorway*). Goodbye.

MRS. BLAUSER. Goodbye.

BALLOU (*to Blauser*). You may come in now.

We see Mr. Blauser with little James on his arm and holding Roger by the hand.

O'DONNELL (*turning to the mother*). Goodbye.

MRS. BLAUSER. Goodbye.

O'Donnell follows Ballou out of the room. Ballou moves from the bedroom to the KITCHEN, followed by O'Donnell, while the family goes into the bedroom. Then Ballou puts his apron on the table as O'Donnell puts down his instruments, while in the BEDROOM we see Mrs. Blauser with the children at her side.

In the KITCHEN, Miss Holtz puts the blood pressure machine and stethoscope in Ballou's bag, shuts it, and brings it over to Ballou who is waiting by the table, as O'Donnell is putting on his coat.

> MISS HOLTZ. Ready, doctor?

Ballou nods and goes through the front door, followed by Holtz and O'Donnell.

On the STAIRWAY, Ballou, followed by Miss Holtz and O'Donnell, comes down the stairs. Then we get a close view of Ballou and O'Donnell in the ALLEY with its garbage depressingly typical of slum conditions.

> O'DONNELL. They were clean decent people. Did you notice the flower boxes they had? . . . And that was a fine baby. . . . But what will happen to him now? We can bring their babies safely . . . but how can we keep them alive?

Ballou, O'Donnell, and Miss Holtz come out of the alley onto DES-PLAINES STREET.

> O'DONNELL (*softly*). Why keep them alive?

Now they are walking on CANAL STREET.

> O'DONNELL. We tell our mothers: Give them plenty of milk to drink. We say: Feed them Cod Liver oil, and orange juice and green vegetables. We say: Keep them clean, and dress them warmly to fight off influenza and pneumonia.

Then they are on the CORNER OF JEFFERSON AND 13TH STREETS, alongside a horribly ramshackle house.

> O'DONNELL. We teach them: The sun will make them strong against rickets and help fight T.B. But where do we tell them to go for the green vegetables? Where do we tell them to move for the sunshine?

They go past the rotten door of the house.

Crosby at camera with Bill Clothier, assistant, lining up night steel-mill shot before dark, Indiana Harbor, May 1939.

O'DONNELL. We say: Guard against measles and whooping cough and scarlet fever and diphtheria. We tell them: We have science to keep your children from being deaf or blind or crippled for life. But where can we tell them to go for the doctors and the science?

They are on MAXWELL STREET, when O'Donnell raises his right hand and stops Ballou, pointing to a close view of the HOUSE, horrible to behold.

O'DONNELL. There is a house in America . . . (*putting his hand down*). They brought them into all our great cities from the hills and fields to build their machines and roll their steel. . . . And left them in these shacks. . . . Here are bad teeth and tainted blood and infected lungs. . . . Here are damaged kidneys and cracked hearts and twisted legs . . .

Ballou looks from the house to O'Donnell, and they start forward again. At the 14TH STREET MARKET, a food truck backs into place.

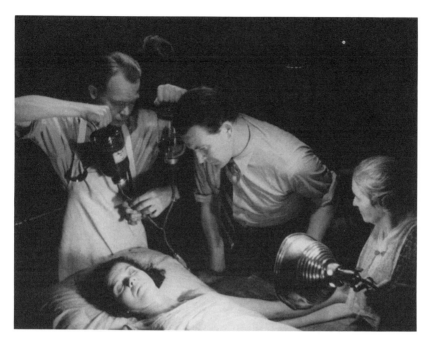

Scene from the final hemorrhage sequence in The Fight for Life. *Left to right: Myron McCormick as Dr. O'Donnell, Will Geer as Dr. Hanson, and Dorothy Urban as the grandmother; Dorothy Adams is the patient.*

O'DONNELL. But here are men who want decent clothes and homes and medical care for their women and children. . . . How can they keep alive in these places?

GLEANERS are picking out food from rubbish. Then appear only the RUBBISH and HANDS taking the food.

O'DONNELL. Here in these markets and warehouses are millions of pounds of surplus food. Yet there are children in this city who never in their lifetime have eaten a decent meal.

More GLEANERS appear at the Market; then the Ballou crew comes down the steps across Market Street. Now the ROOSEVELT BRIDGE appears, with the Ballou crew coming forward.

O'DONNELL (*pointing at the city*). We tell them: "Eat liver," and mark anemia on the record. . . . We tell them: "Rest in bed," and mark cardiac trouble on the record. . . . We tell them: "Eat fresh vegetables," and mark malnutrition on the record. . . . Why don't we just mark on the record: "They're hungry."

A street car stop and side street on ROOSEVELT ROAD: the Ballou crew comes up the side street, and crosses the corner to the street car stop, Ballou talking. Then the STREET CAR comes up, and the crew gets on. The car pulls away and Ballou and O'Donnell are seen looking out the window as now more slum housing appears.

Now BALLOU and O'DONNELL are seen walking.

> BALLOU. Well, it is a time of sadness and trouble; of worn-out ideas and weary people. (*As they stop at the Maternity Center Door*) But since the beginning of medicine, it has been the business of the doctor and the scientist to heal the sick wherever and however he found them. No matter what doubts you have—if you doubt this purpose, you doubt medicine itself.

Miss Holtz goes through the door. O'Donnell takes Ballou's bag and follows him in. The scene dissolves out.

PART FIVE

In the Maternity Center, Effie is taking a call at the SWITCHBOARD.

> EFFIE. Maternity Center . . . Maternity Center . . . Avenue A and 90th St. . . . Yes, Mrs. Donetti—D-O-N-E-T-T-I. . . . Yes, officer . . . we'll send a doctor over right away, officer. (*Turning to Ballou, who has just come in*) Dr. Ballou, emergency call! (*Handing him the slip on which she has copied the name*) The officer says the woman is going blind.

> BALLOU (*calling into the Bulletin Board Room*). Bring the emergency kit, O'Donnell! (*As O'Donnell comes in with a kit and Ballou's bag*) You're not up, but do you want to come?

> O'DONNELL. Sure.

> EFFIE (*as they start toward the door*). It's way out by the steel mills, doctor.

Ballou and O'Donnell come out of the Center and get into the CAR, which drives across, turns onto the drive, and then drives into the woods.

Soon the tall profiles of hotels and office buildings appear, and the car turns onto CHICAGO AVENUE.

We see the Sunset, then a STEEL MILL BRIDGE at dusk as the car cuts across; then AVENUE A in the early evening.

The car draws up at a STEEL SHACK, and Ballou and O'Donnell get out into the night. They enter the shack.

The scene then changes to the Maternity Center SWITCHBOARD, by day, where Effie takes a call.

EFFIE. Maternity Center . . . Maternity Center. . . . Yes, Dr. Ballou. . . . I'll ask Dr. Hanson to join you at the hospital.

Then in the BULLETIN BOARD ROOM a nurse is seen erasing on the board the word "blindness" under "Remarks" opposite the steel shack woman's name and Ballou's and O'Donnell's. She writes instead "Hypertension, hospitalized at Memorial."

Now we see the patient being unloaded from the car by Ballou and O'Donnell at the AMBULANCE ENTRANCE of Memorial Hospital. Here, at an elevator, an intern meets them with a wheelchair and the patient, put into it, is wheeled into the elevator.

In the CORRIDOR outside the patient's room, the nurse, Ballou, O'Donnell and the patient get to the door of her room.

BALLOU (*turning to O'Donnell*). Register the patient, doctor.

Ballou and the nurse wheel the patient into the room.

O'Donnell is now standing near the Head Nurse, who is filling a card out.

NURSE. Name?

O'DONNELL. Mrs. Roberto Donetti.

NURSE. Address?

O'DONNELL. Avenue A and 90th Street.

NURSE. And who's paying for her, doctor?

O'DONNELL. She's on relief. It's a Maternity Center case.

NURSE. Is there a telephone in the house?

O'DONNELL. No. O'Doul's Tavern, Avenue A and 90th Street, is the nearest telephone.

NURSE. Thank you, doctor.

As the nurse looks up, O'Donnell turns and leaves the room. Then he is found hurrying down the hall.

In the PATIENT'S ROOM, we see the woman in a gown or bedjacket. The nurse already has a specimen of urine. O'Donnell enters as Ballou is unwrapping the blood pressure machine.

BALLOU (*to patient*). Have you ever had your blood pressure taken before?

PATIENT. No, sir.

BALLOU. How long have you felt sick?

PATIENT. I just felt awfully sick today, then my eyes went bad.

BALLOU. You went dizzy and you had spots before your eyes?

PATIENT (*as the nurse brings over the syringe for the blood test*). Yes, sir.

BALLOU (taking blood). Have you been to see a doctor during the last few months?

PATIENT. No, sir.

BALLOU (*finishing and handing O'Donnell the test tube as the nurse hands him a flask*). Take these specimens to the lab at once. I've already telephoned.

Ballou starts to take fetal heart tones as O'Donnell leaves. *The Heart Beat becomes audible and is heard in the next scene in the laboratory.*

O'Donnell comes down the hall and turns into the LABORATORY, where we next see him giving specimens to the technician, who takes them to a table and sits down to work, O'Donnell sitting down in a chair against the wall, watching him.

We get another view of the PATIENT'S ROOM with Ballou next to the nurse at the foot of the bed, doing nothing. Then follows the testing in the LABORATORY.

At STATION ONE, in the laboratory, the technician takes five cc. of exalated blood in a pipette and puts it into a flask. Forty-five cc. of the sodium tungstate-sulphuric acid reagent are added with a burette (long, graduated tube with stop-cock at bottom). Flask stoppered and contents thoroughly shaken. He sets the flask down where it must remain from four to five minutes, solution becoming brown. He arranges funnel for filtration.

At STATION TWO, he pours a urinometer cylinder full of urine from the sample bottle, puts in the urinometer, reads the level at which it floats, and writes down his finding of the Specific Gravity.

At STATION ONE he then pours the blood mixture into a funnel and we get a close look at the blood filtering.

At STATION TWO we see urine from the sample bottle being poured into centrifuge tubes and put into the centrifuge. He starts the centrifuge for urinary sediment test.

He pours urine into a test tube from the sample bottle: holds tube over a burner so that top portion of the fluid comes to a boil: holds up tube and a cloud of albumen is apparent. Adds acetic acid in a dropper and again holds up to light. Cloudiness persists. He records the finding.

At STATION ONE, he removes blood filtrate, taking a 5 cc. sample by means of the pipette and putting this into a large test tube.

At STATION TWO, he brings the test tube of blood filtrate and sets it in cotton in the bottom of the glass jar: takes large test tube out of rack and puts it in glass jar also (to prepare standard). 1 cc. of digestion mixture is added to each tube by means of pipette. A small quartz pebble is dropped in blood tube. He reaches over and turns off the centrifuge. He picks up a ring stand at the right and sets tube with blood filtrate over the flame by means of burette clamp. Blood filtrate starts to cook. He removes tube from the centrifuge: pours off supernatant fluid, and removes the residue by means of a dropper and places it on a slide. Walking out with slide, he comes to STATION THREE with the urinary sediment slide and puts it on his microscope. He studies the field and makes a notation.

Back at STATION TWO he covers the blood filtrate tube, which is fuming. One and one half cc. of standard solution is added to standard tube by means of pipette. He reaches for a water flask, Nessler's solution in another flask, a pipette for Nessler's solution and the colorimeter cups. Turns off the flame under blood filtrate tube. Water is added to a standard tube up to 35 cc. mark; water added to the blood filtrate tube up to 35 cc. mark, and the tube is removed from the clamp. It is placed in a jar alongside the other tube, and 15 cc. of Nessler's solution is added to both tubes. Tubes are mixed by inversion, and the colorimeter cups are filled. Then he takes some steps, and next we see him at—

STATION THREE, where he puts cups into the colorimeter, sets standard at 20 mm., and matches the unknown to the known and takes a reading.

Now appears the entire Laboratory Room, with the technician doing tests and writing down the findings.

> NARRATION. *And now the verdict of life or death, written in the chemistry of her blood, is in the hands of ten thousand ghosts. Here she is neither rich nor poor, young nor old. Here she inherits a legacy freely given; all the knowledge of the legions of unknown men of science. A technician in a basement room running a routine test. But he's not alone. . . . He's working with Dobson and Minkowski . . . Fehling and Bright . . . Wolhard and Fahr . . . Benedict and Van Slyke. . . . Working with the unbroken line of men against death, who have labored to make life surer and easier.*

Now, after another view of the PATIENT'S ROOM, where Ballou is taking the pulse, the technician finishes and hands O'Donnell a card as the latter rises. O'Donnell goes out and the technician sits down in the chair to rest.

The scene dissolves to the PATIENT'S ROOM, now lit up, as Ballou is standing at the bed feeling the patient's pulse—nurse on the opposite side. The door opens and O'Donnell enters with the card, and hands it to Ballou, who reads it.

> BALLOU. N.P.N. thirty-five; Albumen two plus; she's got Hyalin and granular casts. Right. (*Taking the stethoscope out of his apron pocket and laying it on a tray, looking at the patient*) We want you to rest and not worry. We're going to keep you here for a little while so you can be quiet. (*As the nurse goes over, picking up Ballou's coat*

and helping him on with it) There's no reason why we shouldn't have a fine baby.

PATIENT. Thank you, doctor.

Ballou and O'Donnell say "goodnight" and leave and the nurse adjusts the bedding and patient for the night.

Ballou and O'Donnell come out of the patient's room into the COR-RIDOR.

BALLOU (*running a hand through his hair*). Here's what we're up against when we have no pre-natal record of our patient. (*As they start walking*) There was no way for us to tell how suddenly that blood pressure hit the ceiling and until we got those tests, there was no way to tell whether she was in a true pre-eclamptic state or whether she was nephritic, due to past sickness that damaged her kidneys—which we found to be the case.

O'DONNELL (*as they reach the corner of the Corridor and stop*). Suppose she'd been in a true pre-eclamptic condition?

They walk to the nurse's desk.

BALLOU. Then she'd have been really blinded or threatening convulsions by the time we got there. (*Giving his orders to the Nurse*) These are the orders for Mrs. Donetti. She must be kept quiet; no visitors. Restrict her fluids to 800 cc. Put her on a salt free diet and record her intake and output. Get a quantitative albumen daily and take a blood pressure every four hours.

HANSON (*entering*). What have we got?

BALLOU. A nephritic. (*Turning to the nurse*) Please notify me of any change in her condition. I'll be in in the morning to see her.

NURSE. Yes, Doctor.

BALLOU (*as he turns and leaves with O'Donnell and Hanson*). She's pretty sick, but we're going to carry her awhile. I think she will be all right.

HANSON. I was afraid she was going to lose her baby when I saw the call. You look all in. How about a cup of coffee?

O'DONNELL. I could use one.

BALLOU. You can drop me off at Presbyterian. There's a post-partum patient there I'm worried about.

O'Donnell looks at Hanson as the scene fades out.

PART SIX

A TENEMENT ROOM at night fades in, with a radio giving the news. Then we see a woman sitting, her profile beside the radio, listening to a few sentences of news. She turns the dial, and then crosses around the table and sits down. O'Donnell looks up from the book he is reading, and the nurse looks up from her sewing. There is music, very soft, and we can hear a fan over it. The nurse and O'Donnell look furtively at the woman and then return to their work, O'Donnell reading, the nurse sewing.

The woman looks around the table at them and pushes her hair back from her face wearily. It is infernally hot and she is slightly wet.

WOMAN (*not looking at anyone, but turning to O'Donnell at the end*). It was cold the last time—almost mid-winter. We had shrimps for supper, I remember. My husband said they were from New Orleans; they fly them in now, he said. They told me the second one would be easier, but she seemed harder than Daniel. Perhaps girls are harder.

O'DONNELL (*smiling at her*). Maybe we'll have a boy this time.

The woman crosses over to the pantry and gets a sack and crosses to the kitchen table. As soon as she rises, O'Donnell looks at the woman and says quietly:

O'DONNELL (*to nurse*). Nurse—

The nurse rises and meets the woman at the kitchen table. The woman gets a short knife out of a drawer and cuts lemons. She hands down a pitcher first from the shelf, and the nurse gets a small piece of ice out of the ice box.

WOMAN. These hot nights, we always have a pitcher made. I forgot tonight—

Now we see the patient's mother, an old woman, sewing, rocking slightly. She peers over at the woman and turns to her sewing.

OLD WOMAN (*to O'Donnell without looking at him*). He went to Detroit two weeks ago. He said there was work there. Things have changed since my day. A man was at home at a time like this. . . .

The woman measures out a little sugar. As she is getting sugar from the shelf we see relief goods known as "Surplus Commodities"—flour sack, or box, or can.

The woman measures out a very little bit of sugar in a tablespoon, which she got out of the drawer along with the knife, and the nurse puts the ice in the pitcher.

WOMAN (*explaining her measuring of the sugar, apologizing with a smile*). Too much sugar just makes you hot again, my husband says. . . .

OLD WOMAN (*still addressing O'Donnell*). You raised your children in a house where there was room. Is there more work, do you think? He said it was better in Detroit.

O'DONNELL (*glancing at her*). I think it's better. We don't know . . . we haven't much time to find out what's going on.

The nurse and the woman are coming over, the nurse carrying the pitcher and glass, the woman carrying glasses. O'Donnell gets up, puts the glasses down, helps the woman into her chair.

O'DONNELL. That looks fine. Thank you.

He smiles at the woman as he is pouring lemonade. The woman looks over at the sleeping medical student, who has accompanied O'Donnell on this case.

WOMAN. I didn't bring one for him. He's sound asleep, isn't he?

O'DONNELL (*cheerfully*). He studies when he's not out on a case— that's why he's so sleepy.

The woman drinks part of the lemonade, and wipes the hair from her face. She looks toward the bedroom.

WOMAN. . . . . they're quiet tonight.

She rises and walks toward the bedroom.

In the CHILDREN'S BEDROOM we see the sleeping children, and the woman looking at them and then returning to the kitchen. Then she goes to her bedroom, walking slowly to the table. She keeps on walking back and forth now in the KITCHEN as the nurse times her and O'Donnell continues to read. She glances at the clock, stops hesitantly by the table, is taken slowly with pain and holds on to the chair.

O'DONNELL (*rising and catching her*). Well, that was a good one.

O'Donnell and the nurse take her by the arms.

O'DONNELL (*looking over his shoulder as they start for the bedroom*). Scrub up, doctor—

They walk into the bedroom. The student wakes up, rubs his eyes, and goes over to the sink, while O'Donnell, going out with the patient, at the door makes a sign to the Old Woman to stay in the kitchen.

In the BEDROOM O'Donnell and the nurse help the patient to bed. The nurse stays with the patient and O'Donnell walks back to the kitchen.

In the KITCHEN, the Old Woman in the rocking chair watches the student scrub up. O'Donnell enters, puts on cap and mask, and watches the student to see that he is scrubbing up properly, the Old Woman in the rocking chair observing.

Now O'Donnell is with the patient in the BEDROOM as the nurse brings in a pan of Lysol and a pan of bichloride. On the last trip she has her cap and mask on. The patient's face is very tense as fetal heart beats are taken.

O'DONNELL. Take the fetal heart beats, doctor. Be careful with those hands! Remember the island of safety.

The student's finger is beating out the heart tones. (*The sound of a ticking metronome starts with the student's heart tone beat.*)

In the KITCHEN we note the old fashioned cabinet clock, and the Old Woman rocking in the chair. Suddenly she stops rocking. Then only the pendulum of the clock is visible.

Outside on the TENEMENT STOOP, Negroes in the shadow are playing a guitar and a banjo. A policeman walks past the houses. He passes two men on a step—one is playing a guitar, the other listening to him. Then he comes to the tenement stoop. A man is sitting there with a bottle of beer. Dim light shows through the transom of an open door of the patient's house. The cop stops by the man with the beer.

POLICEMAN. What's going on up there?

MAN'S VOICE. Just a woman having a baby.

The policeman walks on past the dim-lit doorway.

The scene dissolves to a close view of the new-born baby. Then we see it being weighed, O'Donnell, the student and the old woman disclosed.

O'DONNELL (*putting the baby down and turning to the Old Woman*). Eight pounds—I was off a quarter of a pound. You can take him in now.

The nurse picks him up and she and the Old Woman leave. O'Donnell turns to the student as the Old Woman carries the baby into the BEDROOM.

The Old Woman puts the baby in the bed beside the mother, who is looking at it.

The nurse and Dr. O'Donnell are now packing; the student still filling out the report.

O'DONNELL. Now, have we checked the seven points?

STUDENT. Yes, sir. Baby in good condition. Mother uninjured. Blood pressure a hundred and ten over seventy, temperature ninety-eight-four, pulse normal.

O'DONNELL. That's fine. You see, our plan of delivery here was very simple, doctor. Our patient is a young woman. She's had two children already. She has a normal pelvis. Position of the baby was normal. We had a spontaneous delivery. Fill out the birth certificate.

At the SWITCHBOARD at night, Effie takes a call.

Returning to the TENEMENT, we see the Baby.

OLD WOMAN. Do you want anything?

WOMAN. No, I'm fine, thank you.

At the SWITCHBOARD, Effie gets up and goes to the BULLETIN BOARD ROOM. There she goes to the Bulletin board, wipes off the last report on O'Donnell's case, and writes: "Delivered. Mother and baby O.K. Male, 8 pounds."

In the tenement KITCHEN, the student puts the record in his bag and takes off his apron, while O'Donnell strolls toward the bedroom.

The Old Woman is sitting in the BEDROOM with her daughter and the baby in bed. As O'Donnell strolls in, the patient smiles weakly at him. She looks very bad. O'Donnell takes her pulse, then quickly starts to throw the bed covers back. He rushes to the door.

O'DONNELL (*in the doorway facing the kitchen*). Hemorrhage!

He rushes back from the doorway and grabs the stethoscope. The Old Woman jumps up. The student and the nurse come in from the kitchen, nurse bringing the bag with her, and placing it on the table. O'Donnell takes the baby from the bed and hands him to the Old Woman.

O'DONNELL. Take him into the other room.

O'Donnell, student and nurse are crowded around the bed, as the Old Woman goes to the kitchen with the baby.

O'DONNELL. Pituitrin! Let me have it, nurse. Let me have it.

The nurse gives him a hypo, and O'Donnell injects pituitrin.

O'DONNELL. Syringe!

O'Donnell wraps the blood pressure wrapping around the patient's arm as a tourniquet, the student pumping the pressure.

We see blood going from the syringe into a test tube.

O'DONNELL (*to the student*). Report to the Center immediately—then rush this specimen over to the blood bank and hurry! (*To nurse, as the Student says "Yes, sir," and leaves.*) Collect all the jars and bottles in the place, and put lots of water on to boil.

NURSE (*going to the kitchen*). Yes, sir.

In the Maternity Center we see Effie at the SWITCHBOARD taking a call; then Ballou reading in the light of one lamp in his room as his phone rings. Ballou becomes tense immediately when he answers.

BALLOU. What's her pulse? Blood pressure? Right. Well, get going! (*Jiggling the receiver*) Effie, call Dr. Hanson downstairs at once!

He hangs up, grabs his coat from the back of the chair, and dashes out of the room.

Now Ballou dashes down the stairs and past Effie, his hat in his hand.

BALLOU. Hemorrhage on O'Donnell's case!

Effie jumps up from the switchboard and runs after him into the BULLETIN BOARD ROOM. Then Ballou and Effie run through toward the bag room. Here Ballou and Effie get out the hemorrhage kits from the Emergency Kit Cupboard. Effie taking the small box and the operating lamp, Ballou the big bags.

Ballou and Effie hurl hemorrhage kits on a table. He goes to the card index file as Effie turns on the light.

BALLOU. Phone the blood bank that Harris is on his way over.

As Effie dashes out Ballou gets a card from the desk and studies it under the lamp, Effie's voice on the phone coming over.

EFFIE'S VOICE. Hello . . . give me the blood bank. Hello, this is the Maternity Center. We have a patient in shock. Dr. Harris is on his way over with blood specimen now. Thank you.

Ballou, having finished studying the card, while adjusting his tie and collar, goes to Bulletin Board, erases the report of "Delivered O.K." on the O'Donnell case, and scrawls "Post-partum hemorrhage," his own name and Hanson's.

Hanson rolls downstairs into the SWITCHBOARD ROOM, trying to put on his coat, obviously just awakened.

HANSON. What have we got?

EFFIE. Hemorrhage—O'Donnell case.

Ballou enters from the Bulletin Board room, carrying all the hemorrhage kits. Hanson grabs the operating light and the big emergency bag. Ballou has his bag and small flat case.

HANSON. What about blood?

BALLOU. Harris is on his way now.

HANSON. Let's go!

They leave, Ballou first, Effie holding the door.

Now we are in the Tenement. In the KITCHEN the nurse is collecting jars and bottles and stoking the stove.

In the BEDROOM, O'Donnell finishes taking blood pressure. He leaves wrapping on the woman's arm and turns to the nurse.

O'DONNELL (*under his breath*). Sixty over twenty—ergot.

The nurse prepares and hands him ergot. He injects it in the patient's arm. The patient's face reveals shock.

WOMAN. You won't let me die, will you, doctor?

O'DONNELL (*seen closely*). No. . . . No! (*Injecting morphine*) Adrenalin!

He administers adrenalin, then takes the blood pressure as the nurse goes out.

Ballou and Hanson enter the KITCHEN, throw down their kits and hats, and dash right into the bedroom.

O'Donnell looks up from taking the blood pressure as Ballou and Hanson enter the BEDROOM, where the Old Woman is watching at the foot of the bed.

O'DONNELL (*Ballou and Hanson near him*). Pulse sixty. Blood pressure sixty over zero.

HANSON (*turning to the nurse*). Fix the operative set-up.

BALLOU (*turning to O'Donnell as the Old Woman and the nurse go out*). What have you done?

O'DONNELL. I've given her pituitrin, ergot, morphine, and I've just administered adrenalin.

Ballou takes the patient's pulse.

BALLOU (*turning to O'Donnell*). Massage her.

Ballou turns away, puts down his coat, and rolls up his sleeves, while Hanson walks out. Ballou comes back, and stands next to O'Donnell and the patient.

The nurse goes over to the table in the KITCHEN, and starts unpacking a bag as Hanson comes in. Then she is seen turning to the stove and putting saline in hot water.

HANSON (*to the Old Woman as he pulls up chairs*). Get me the ironing board, mother.

The old woman puts an ironing board across chairs and covers it with newspapers. Ballou enters, goes to the sink, and starts scrubbing. Hanson walks into the bedroom. In the BEDROOM O'Donnell and Hanson lift the patient up and carry her into the KITCHEN. Here Hanson and O'Donnell get the patient on the table, the operative set-up being prepared while Ballou is scrubbing up. The nurse has plugged in the light next to the radio and hands it to the Old Woman.

HANSON (*to the nurse*). Prepare the glucose and saline. (*Getting the patient arranged*) Glucose, nurse.

We see the hands of the nurse plugging in glucose. Then O'Donnell puts the needle in the patient's arm—starts glucose while Hanson holds tourniquet on the patient's arm, then takes glucose container from the nurse and holds it.

Ballou having finished putting on gloves at the sink, comes over to the operative table and stoops to pick something up.

BALLOU. All right, nurse.

Ballou's and the nurse's hands are going through the action of pledgets and forceps and gauze. The nurse and Hanson and O'Donnell are at the patient's head, watching Ballou who is working on her.

The student comes through the door with blood, and goes to the head of the table.

HANSON. Give her the blood.

O'Donnell and the nurse put the blood container on its tube, and clamp off the glucose, O'Donnell holding the flask of blood. Now a hand wipes perspiration from the patient's forehead, and the group is waiting in suspense—someone is taking the patient's pulse. Blood is draining out of a glass to the accompaniment of music and the sound of the Heart Beat.

The scene slowly dissolves to a street with a church seen in the light of dawn. It is dawn in the BEDROOM too. The patient is in bed, everybody watching her, relieved, except for the nurse and the student who are cleaning up in the kitchen.

O'DONNELL (*finishing blood pressure*). One hundred over fifty.

O'Donnell looks down and smiles at the patient. We see her face. The perspiration is gone and she is out of shock and recovering. She smiles at O'Donnell, who smiles back at her.

BALLOU (*smiling at the woman as he puts on his coat*). We'll call in this afternoon.

They say "goodbye" and walk into the kitchen, leaving O'Donnell to leave last.

Hanson steps to the Old Woman, who is sitting in the rocking chair in the KITCHEN.

HANSON. You can go in now, it's all right.

OLD WOMAN. Thank you.

O'DONNELL (*to Ballou*). Well, I guess I'd better report to the Center.

BALLOU. Fine.

He leaves, but Ballou stops at the sink to instruct the student—

BALLOU. Take her blood pressure every hour. We'll be back again late this afternoon.

STUDENT. Yes, sir.

O'Donnell looks at the baby in its crib, and goes out for his coat.

The scene dissolves to the MATERNITY CENTER at night. Effie is asleep, but the telephone rings and awakens her.

EFFIE. Maternity Center . . . Maternity Center. . . . Oh, I'm glad, Doctor O'Donnell.

O'Donnell, Hanson and Ballou come down the TENEMENT STEPS outside. It is dawn. They throw their bags in the car, O'Donnell has one foot on the running board.

BALLOU. How about a cup of coffee?

O'DONNELL. I'd like to drop off at Memorial first. I've a patient there I'm worried about.

At this echo of Ballou's line after the nephritic case, Ballou and Hanson exchange glances. They get into the car and drive off. We get glimpses of the early sun, and of people going to work as the car disappears down the street. Then the scene fades out.

BIBLIOGRAPHY

1. "Microbe Hunters," "Men Against Death," "Why Keep Them Alive?" "The Fight for Life," "Health Is Wealth," Paul de Kruif, published by Harcourt, Brace & Co.
2. "Principles and Practice of Obstetrics," Jos. B. De Lee, A.M.M.D., Saunders, 1938.
3. "Biology of Death," Raymond Pearl, J. P. Lippincott, 1920.
4. "The Phenomenon of Life," George Washington Crile.
5. "Hypertension," Dr. Fishberg.
6. Dr. Boyd on Heart Disease (Essay).
7. Children's Bureau Publication No. 246: Proceedings of Conference on Better Care for Mothers and Babies.
   Sect: "The Need Today," Report of Surgeon General Parran: Report of Dr. Jennings Litzenberg, M.D., University of Minnesota Medical School.
   Sect: "What Is Being Done Today," Report of Dr. Beatrice E. Tucker.
8. Report on Stillbirths and Infant Mortality, U.S. Department of Commerce, Bureau of the Census.
9. Report of the Technical Committee on Medical Care: "The

Need for a National Health Program," pp. 5–11, Sect. from pp. 21–28. "Income and Health Needs." Summary 34–36.

10. "Who Can Afford Health?" Pamphlet No. 27, 1939, Public Affairs Committee.

11. "Doctors, Dollars and Disease," Pamphlet No. 10, 1938, Public Affairs Committee.

12. Report of the Committee on the Cost of Medical Care, 28 vs., Public Affairs Committee.

13. "Consumer Incomes in the United States: Their Distribution in 1935–36," a report published in 1938 by the National Resources Planning Board.

14. "Consumer Expenditures in the United States," a report published in 1939 by the National Resources Planning Board.

EPILOGUE

I hope this account of mine will give the readers some idea of where I came from, what I tried to do, what I did, and what happened.

I have witnessed images beginning with sitting in the first movie theater in Buckhannon, West Virginia, and regarding Mr. and Mrs. John Bunny, Tom Mix, and Charlie Chaplin, and I have lived to see images on the television screen of men walking on the moon and cavorting around in capsules in outer space. I have witnessed the motion picture companies devouring the theatre, and I have witnessed electronic and newspaper conglomerates devouring the movie industry, and I expect soon to see new electronic images bounce around from land to outer space and back on a large home screen. But musing over this electronic age that lies ahead of us, I am reminded of Thoreau, who, told about the coming of Western Union, and that "Now it is possible for Maine to talk to Texas," replied: "Yes, but what if Maine doesn't have anything to say to Texas?"

I think often, also, of my outrage, but agreement, with a flip comment Eddie Cantor made years ago during a radio show. He said: "America is that place between New York and Hollywood."

Almost all our image oracles are word men who *talk* about images rather than exhibiting them, and they are paid indecent wages for so doing.

I saw these same men in my childhood days—a pushcart lit by a kerosene flame—the cart full of junk—a monkey on a string—a huckster's monologue—a jerk to pull the monkey on the string when some cash was paid in—same men. Except now they have pushed their carts into our homes.

I have lived through hard times in the hills of West Virginia and again in the canyons of New York City. I have more than once recalled the hardships my paternal grandfather Mifflin Lorentz, whom I never knew, went through in his lifetime. Although he was the first county clerk in Upshur County, Virginia, and had the best home on Main Street and was a man described by a local historian as being of "ruffles and flourishes," because of the Civil War he was disfranchised and deprived of his right to practice law, to hold office, and to vote. He had freed his slaves before the Civil War, but he was against the secession of West Virginia from Virginia, and he made a speech on the courthouse steps, surrounded by friends with cocked pistols, denouncing the occasion by President Lincoln of creating a new state. He then was helped out of town by an armed escort.

His home was burned to the ground by General Imboden's raiders.

He came back to now *West* Virginia and married a young, petite girl who was a friend of his grown daughters, went up into the hills in the remote settlement of Falls Mills on the Little Kanawha River, set up a mill and a general store, and raised three good children before he died.

I have thought often of an educated lawyer starting over in such a remote area and the heritage of courage he left his children and his widow. These things always kept me going when times have been rough.

Recently a historian sent me a clipping from a Braxton County newspaper which had an account of how a Mr. Camden had been told by President Grover Cleveland that he, the president, wanted a quiet place, far from anybody, where he could sit and think and go fishing. Mr. Camden recommended that he go to Falls Mills, Braxton County, West Virginia, and visit my grandfather Mifflin. The story goes on to say that the arrangements were made but were never carried out, as the roads from Weston to Falls Mills were completely impassable. It would appear that impoverished and disfranchised as he was, grandfather Mifflin was still considered by some high authorities as being a man of some importance and influence.

Once again I have been living in a "come-and-get-it" culture in our country. There were obvious unnecessary regulations passed during the New Deal and war times, but we have deregulated almost every sensible regulation (including the Ten Commandments) so that food, drugs, water, banks, aircraft, roads, bridges—you name it—periodically are called unsafe.

Last year an old acquaintance who had retired after serving a congressman as an administrative assistant for many years sent me a letter in which he discussed the concerns he had for our country. He expressed them so well that I take the liberty of quoting one paragraph from his letter:

Pare Lorentz at work in his study, Armonk, New York, November 1989.
Photograph by Elizabeth Lorentz.

It occurs to me that possibly the cast of governmental characters in those Depression and War years, loom larger than those we have today, as it was all new then—it wasn't as large then, the country was just starting on the path of government guidance and all things seemed honest, good and possible. Some fifty to fifty-five years and countless thousands of bureaucrats later, it is difficult to even remember the promise of those beginnings in the greed spattered reality of the immediate past and the present.

Amen.

What follows is a brief listing of Pare Lorentz's major
accomplishments and honors.

Film Critic:
  Judge magazine, 1926–34
  New York Evening Journal, 1931–32
  Vanity Fair magazine, 1932–33
  Town and Country magazine, 1933–36
  McCall's magazine, 1935–41

Books:
  Censored: The Private Life of the Movies
  co-authored with Morris L. Ernst
  published by Cape & Smith, 1930

  The Roosevelt Year
  published by Funk & Wagnalls, 1934

  The River
  published by Stackpole & Sons, 1938

  Lorentz on Film: Movies 1927–1941
  published by Hopkinson and Blake, 1975
  reissued by University of Oklahoma Press, 1988

  FDR's Moviemaker: Memoirs and Scripts
  published by University of Nevada Press, 1992

Films:
  The Plow That Broke the Plains (1936)
  written and directed for the U.S. Resettlement
  Administration

  The River (1938)
  written and directed for the USDA Farm Security
  Administration
  released by Paramount Pictures; won World Prize
  at the Venice Film Festival for best documentary;
  also received the Grant Shorts Award from Jay
  Emanuel Publications

The Fight for Life (1940)
written and directed for the U.S. Film Service
released by Columbia Pictures; won Best Documentary Film Award from the National Board of Review
script included in *Twenty Best Film Plays*, a book
by Prof. John Gassner and Dudley Nichols (Crown
Publishers, 1943)

1938–39
member, Inter-American Affairs Committee,
representing radio and motion pictures for the
U.S. Department of State

1938–40
chief of U.S. Film Service, appointed by
President Franklin D. Roosevelt

1940–41
National Defense Editor, *McCall's* magazine

May 1942
presidential appointment as major, U.S. Army Air
Corps

1943–46
commanding officer, Overseas Technical Unit,
ATC; advanced to rank of Lieutenant Colonel,
U.S. Air Force

September 1945
awarded Legion of Merit

1946–47
chief of films, Theater and Music, Civil Affairs
Division, U.S. War Department; in charge of
those subjects in occupied countries

1947–78
president, treasurer, Pare Lorentz Associates,
Inc., 166 E. 74th Street, New York, NY
10021

1955
>   special correspondent to the *Washington Post*
>   during the first United Nations Conference on
>   Peaceful Uses of the Atom at Geneva, Switzerland

Special Honors:
>   Centennial of U.S. Department of Agriculture
>   Reception and Award (1963)
>
>   Pare Lorentz Film Festival at the National
>   Archives (1970)
>
>   Honorary Professor of Speech, University of
>   Wisconsin, Oshkosh (1971)
>
>   Honorary Doctor of Letters, West Virginia
>   Wesleyan (1972)
>
>   Honorary Doctor of Humanities, West Virginia
>   University (1978)
>
>   Honors Reception, National Audiovisual Center
>   (1979)
>
>   "Sadie" Award for "outstanding contributions . . .
>   field of education," Birmingham International
>   Educational Film Festival (1980)
>
>   Special Salute for *The Plow That Broke the Plains*
>   and *The River*, Academy of Motion Picture Arts
>   and Sciences (1981)
>
>   First Annual Career Achievement Award of the
>   International Documentary Association, presented
>   by David L. Wolper (1985)
>
>   The Washington Film Council First Annual Award
>   of Honor, in recognition of fifty years of creative
>   contributions to the art of the film (1986)
>
>   Lifetime Achievement Award, presented by the
>   West Virginia Division of Culture and History
>   (1990)

ACKNOWLEDGMENTS I hereby thank the organizations and the individuals who have given me permission to quote from their published works and public statements about me and my work:

for the eight lines of the Yeats poem from *The Poems of W. B. Yeats: A New Edition* edited by Richard J. Finneran (New York: Macmillan, 1983) which I have used in the dedication to my wife Elizabeth;

for permission to republish the gracious and lucid words used by Commissioner Drennen in his speech to the opening audience of the Pare Lorentz exhibition of his documentary films;

to the William Morris Agency for permission to use part of Professor John Gassner's introductory essay "Documentary Films as Literature" from the out-of-print book *Twenty Best Film Plays*, edited by John Gassner and Dudley Nichols, Crown Publishers, New York, 1943;

to Elaine Steinbeck and her representative Julie Fallowfield for their permissions;

and most gratitude to Mrs. Rauni Swan for her intelligent and continuous work on my behalf during the past four years of working on this manuscript, having to take time out from her household responsibilities . . . my deepest thanks.

:   :   :

I also wish to thank the people who approved of my work in peacetime and in wartime and who stood by me when I got into bureaucratic difficulties;

James D. LeCron of Des Moines, Iowa, originally a French Huguenot from Chambersburg, Pa. Jim encouraged every step I took in moviemaking in Washington;

Arch A. Mercey, who was in charge of my Washington office, such as it was, and extremely knowledgeable of the protocol of necessary paperwork, all of which he handled;

John Franklin Carter, my superior in the office of information of the Resettlement Administration;

Robert H. Jackson, attorney general of the United States, later assistant justice of the Supreme Court and also chief prosecutor at the Nuremberg trials;

Gordon Clapp, who rose to be chief of the TVA;

David Lilienthal, his boss, who became head of the Atomic Energy Commission;

Miss Elizabeth Roberts, whom I chose from the typing pool in Washington to be my secretary because she was intelligent and diligent;

J. D. Ross, who was slated to become the chief of the Columbia River Valley Authority; the coming of the war delayed the appointment;

Adrian Fischer, legal advisor to the secretary of State and then general counsel of the Atomic Energy Commission under David Lilienthal;

Roark Bradford and Lyle Savon, and King Vidor, the old-timer who sent me Floyd Crosby as a cameraman, and Lloyd Nosler, one of the best film editors in Hollywood, both of whom served under me in the Overseas Technical Unit during World War II;

John M. Carmody, who as head of the REA cajoled me into producing "Power and the Land" for REA. He was later made head of the Federal Works Agency and helped me immensely to make arrangements to photograph construction work at the Bonneville and Grand Coulee dams;

Surgeon General Thomas Parran, who started his political career working on TB as a medical director under Governor Franklin D. Roosevelt. He was later appointed surgeon general by Roosevelt and was the best surgeon general in the long history of the organization;

Dr. Paul de Kruif and Surgeon General Parran were intimate friends. De Kruif and Don Brace (partner in Harcourt, Brace publishers) gave me out-of-hand all the dramatic rights to Paul's book *The Fight for Life*, which Harcourt, Brace had published;

Morris L. Cooke of Chestnut Hill, Philadelphia. He had been a troubleshooter for President Woodrow Wilson and he became one for FDR. He arranged, against my will, for me to give one of the Bok lectures in the Academy of Music where he informed me, as I took a seat in an old, paint-peeled, green dressing room, that this was the Academy where Abraham Lincoln had accepted his second nomination for the presidency. That left me full of fear and trembling for the rest of the evening, although the exhibition of *The River* did meet with some startled applause;

John Houseman, my next door neighbor at the time, who reciprocated some of my advice by giving me some good advice himself;

D. J. Ward, business manager for the Resettlement Administration and former U.S. Marine who stuck with me even though he was bewildered at my activities;

Paul Jordan, the field representative of the Office of Information on Resettlement and later Farm Security, for exhibiting and booking my films in the Midwest and West Coast independent theaters; Dean Jennings, a good writer who worked on the West Coast;

and the chief executive of the U.S. government who looked at all the work for which I was responsible and finally made me responsible for *all* motion picture operations in and about the federal government—my biggest fan and the most steadfast government employee—four times elected president of the U.S., Franklin D. Roosevelt.

INDEX

Agha, Dr., 29
Agriculture, Department of, 36–37, 77, 109, 141, 152. *See also* Farm Security Administration; Resettlement Administration
Alexander, Will, 54, 108
Alsop, Joseph, 149, 150
American Association of Advertising Agencies, 11
Anthony, Norman, 14, 16, 17

Balaban, Barney, 108
Barrymore, John, 26
Bates, Sarah Richardson, 24–25
Bell, Miriam, 130–131
Benaron, Henry, 138, 143–144
Benchley, Robert, 10, 137–138
Berry, Iris, 78
Brace, Don, 136
Bradford, Roark, 56, 57, 58
Bridgeman, John S., 130–131
Brokaw, Clare Boothe, 27, 28
Broun, Heywood, 22, 35
Bruce, Ned, 116, 117
Bull, Harry, 30
Bushwea, Percy, 25
Butler, Smedley, 14–15

Cagney, James, 113–115
Carter, John Franklin, 36, 53, 108
CBS. *See* Columbia Broadcasting System
Censored: The Private Life of the Movies, 20–22

Chalmers, Thomas Hardie, 40, 53–54
Chaplin, Charlie, 15, 118–119, 138
Chicago Tribune, 133, 135
Clair, René, 25
Clothier, William, 133
Columbia Broadcasting System (CBS), 77, 78–80
Connelly, Joe, 23–24, 25, 30–31, 34, 36
Cooke, Alistair, 79
Corcoran, Tom, 55–56, 77, 79, 80, 116, 140, 154
Crosby, Floyd, 117, 127, 133, 134, 136, 139
Crowninshield, Frank, 29
Curley, Bill, 25–26

Davies, Marion, 24
de Kruif, Paul, 124–125, 127, 131, 135, 136, 142, 159. *See also Fight for Life, The*
de Kruif, Rhea, 146
De Lee, Joseph B., 125, 144, 151, 159, 161
De Mott, Robert, 108
Dieterle, William, 114
Digges, Dudley, 126–127, 143, 195
Disney, Walt, 57

Early, Steve, 134
Ecce Homo, 77–82, 122, 124, 151; script, 83–104
"Ecce Homo" (radio program), 77, 78–80, 117, 120–121

Edison, Thomas, 12
Edison Mazda Lamp Company, 12
Edison Sales Builder, The, 11–16
Education, Department of, 140, 141,
    152
Ernst, Morris L., 20–22, 23, 32

Farm Security Administration, 53,
    108
Federal Security Agency, 140
Fight for Life, The, 124–163; Chi-
    cago events, 132–139, 146–148;
    Digges in, 126–127, 195; distribu-
    tion of, 149–155, 158–163; fund-
    ing problems, 139–143; script,
    164–225
Fishbein, Morris, 159–160
Fischer, John, 53, 54, 108, 109
Flaherty, Robert, 78, 141, 152
Ford, Corey, 10
Ford, John, 138
Fox, William, 18, 19

Gannett, Lewis, 81
Geer, Will, 163
General Electric, 12–13, 14, 16
George, Harold L., 105
Gercke, George, 54, 55
Gilliam, Laurence, 79
Gilman, Mildred, 34–35
Goldwyn, Samuel, 56, 119
Grapes of Wrath, The (Steinbeck),
    106, 107, 120–121, 128–129,
    138–139
Grierson, John, 78
Griswold, Oliver, 162–163
Gruenberg, Louis, 143, 145, 146–
    147
Guthrie, Woody, 163

Harding, Warren G., 21–22
Hawks, Bill, 114
Haynes, Storrs, 128
Hays, Will, 21–22, 57, 141
Hearst, William Randolph, 23, 24,
    25, 30, 36
Hecht, Ben, 26
Hellinger, Mark, 3–4
Herrmann, Bernard, 78, 120
Hitchcock, Alfred, 25, 57
Hoover, Herbert, 13
Houghton, William Morris, 17, 18
Howe, Louis, 51
Hunter, Howard, 136, 137
Huston, John, 136

Ickes, Harold, 154
Indian Bureau, 51
In Dubious Battle (Steinbeck), 108,
    109, 112–115
Ingersoll, Ralph, 10
Ivens, Joris, 141, 152

Jackson, Joseph Henry, 110, 117
Johnson, George E. Q., 134
Johnson, Nunnally, 106, 138–139,
    145
Judge, 14–15, 16, 17–19, 27, 30

Kettering, Charles Franklin, 161
Kissack, Robert, 108

Land, The, 141, 152
Lange, Dorothea, 33, 43, 122
Lanning, 56, 143
Le Cron, James, 35, 36
Lee, Robert E., 58–59
LeRoy, Mervyn, 112
Lewis, Bill, 77, 78–79, 80

Lindley, Dan, 40–41
Lindley, Peggy, 40–41, 161
Little, Mildred, 7–8
Lorentz, Alma MacTaggart Ruttencutter, 4
Lorentz, Pare, 1–2, 3–11. *See also specific publications, movies and topics*
Lorentz, Pare Hanson, 4, 7
Lorentz on Film, 112

MacArthur, Charles, 26
McCall's Magazine, 52, 78
McCormick, Myron, 143
McGowan, Frank, 160–161
McIver, 12, 13, 14, 15, 16
McNutt, Paul V., 140, 154
MacTaggart, Leonard. *See* Lorentz, Pare
Mellett, Lowell, 82, 133, 147, 154
Mercey, Arch, 82
Miller, Alexander, 161, 162
Morgenthau, Henry, 116–117, 142, 150
Muni, Paul, 113
Murnau, F. W., 18, 19, 42

National Emergency Council, 82, 133, 140
National Industrial Recovery Act (NIRA), 35
National Mazda Lamp Company, 12
Newsweek, 30, 31
New York County Medical Society, 161–162
New Yorker, The, 5, 10–11
New York Evening Journal, 23–26
Night Flight (Saint-Exupéry), 41–42

NIRA. *See* National Industrial Recovery Act
Nosler, Lloyd, 52–53, 124, 147, 152, 155
Nugent, Frank, 139

Of Mice and Men (Steinbeck), 110, 112
Olson, Culbert L., 142
Otis, Elizabeth, 107, 108, 113

Pare Lorentz and the Documentary Film (Snyder), 38
Parran, Thomas, 125–126, 142
Pearson, Drew, 32, 34
Peet, Max, 144–145, 159–160
Pelswick, Rose, 24
Plain Talk, 14
Player, William O., Jr., 141
Plow That Broke the Plains, The, 30, 38, 39–43, 46, 49, 81; script, 44–45, 47–48, 50
Power and the Land, 141, 152

Ratcliff, Jack, 9, 30
Reorganization Act of 1939, 140
Resettlement Administration, 36–38, 53, 108. *See also specific movies*
River, The, 39, 51–59, 78, 81, 110–111; script, 60–76
Roberts, Elizabeth, 116
Robson, Bill, 77, 78, 79, 80, 120
Rockefeller, Nelson, 29
Rogers, Will, 15
Roosevelt, Eleanor, 54, 141–142, 147–148, 149, 161
Roosevelt, Franklin D., 34, 125; and Resettlement Administration films, 51, 53, 54–56, 77, 79, 80–81; and

Fight for Life, The, 149–152; and U.S. Film Service funding, 140, 142–143
Roosevelt Year, The, 28–29, 35
Rosa, Phil, 14
Ross, Harold, 10–11
Ross, J. D., 82
Rowe, James, 140, 142
Rural Electrification Administration, 141, 152
Ruttencutter, John, 3, 6

Savage, Joe, 9
Sawyer, Gordon, 56, 143
Saxon, Lyle, 56, 57
Scribner's, 16
Sea of Cortez, The (Steinbeck), 147
Semmelweis, Ignaz, 125
Shane, Ted, 10
Sherwood, Robert, 10
Simpson, Walt, 161
Smallens, Alexander, 39–40, 54
Smith, C. R., 105
Smith, Harold D., 141–142
Snyder, Robert L., 38
Sobel, Bernie, 15
Soviet Union, 34, 35
Steinbeck, Carol, 108, 117–118, 121, 131, 143
Steinbeck, Gwyn, 145–146, 158
Steinbeck, John, 105–111, 117–124, 128–130, 138–139; health problems, 143–145; *In Dubious Battle* project, 108, 109, 112–115; remarriage, 145–146, 158; *Fight for Life, The*, 130–131, 137–138, 147, 152–153, 155, 158; and U.S. Film Service funding, 141–143
Steinmetz, Charles Proteus, 13

Stimson, Henry L., 105, 106
Studebaker, John S., 140, 142, 154
Sullivan, Gael, 133–134
Sunrise (Murnau), 18, 19, 42
Supreme Court, 52, 53

Taylor, Paul, 122
They Won't Forget, 112
Thomson, Virgil, 38, 39–40, 52, 53, 58, 78
To the Pure (Ernst), 20
Town and Country, 30
Treasury, Department of the, 116
Trilby, 26
Tucker, Beatrice, 131, 144
Tugwell, Rexford Guy, 36–37, 38, 51, 53, 54, 108

U.S. Camera, 43
U.S. Film Service, 77–78, 80, 82, 117, 140, 142, 145, 154. *See also specific movies*
Untermeyer, Samuel, 12

van Dongen, Helen, 152
Vanity Fair, 26–28, 29–30
Veteran's bonus army march, 34
Vidor, Betty, 111
Vidor, King, 53, 77, 78, 111

Wagner, Max, 145
Wagner, Robert F., 35
Wallace, Henry A., 35, 36, 122, 123
Warner Brothers, 132, 136–137
Warner, Jack, 137
"Washington Merry-Go-Round, The," 32
"Washington Side Show, The," 31, 32, 33–38

Wegner, Dr., 135

White, Katherine (Mrs. E. B.), 10

Whitney, John Hay, 28

Wiese, Otis, 52, 146

Williams, Annie Laurie, 107, 108, 113

Williamson, Sam, 30

Winchell, Walter, 3

Woods, George, 124–125

Working Days (Steinbeck), 108

World-Telegram, 22

World War II, 105, 127, 141, 143, 151–152, 154

Wylie, Phil, 10

"Young Man Goes to Work, A," 16

Zanuck, Daryl F., 138

Zochling, Leo, 40